Leaving Certific
Higher Level

Excellence in English Language

Paper 1

Cathy Sweeney

First published 2014

Educate.ie

Walsh Educational Books Ltd

Castleisland

Co. Kerry

Ireland

www.educate.ie

ISBN 978-1-910052-04-4

Associate Editor: Jennifer Armstrong

Design and Cover: Kieran O'Donoghue

Layout: Compuscript

Printed and Bound in Ireland by Walsh Colour Print, Castleisland, Co. Kerry

PERMISSION ACKNOWLEDGEMENTS

Just Kids: © Patti Smith, 2011, *Just Kids*, Bloomsbury Publishing Plc • Margaret Laurence, 'Where the World Began': By permission of AP Watt at United Artists on behalf of New End • *The Speckled People* by Hugo Hamilton: Reprinted by permission of HarperCollins Publishers Ltd, © 2003, Hugo Hamilton • Neil Gaiman 'Princess and some thoughts on writing': Neil Gaiman, 2013 • Dennis O'Driscoll, Stepping Stones: Reproduced by kind permission of Faber and Faber Ltd • Stephen Fry, 'An Open Letter ...': © 2011 Stephen Fry • Anonymous, *A Woman in Berlin*: Virago, an imprint of Little, Brown Book Group • Anonymous, *A Woman in Berlin (Eine Frau in Berlin)*: Tagebuchaufzeichnungen vom 20 April bis 22 Juni 1945 © 2002 Hannelore Marek, © AB – Die Andere Bibliothek GmbH & Co. KG, Berlin 2011 (First published by Eichborn Verlag, Frankfurt am Main 2003) • Lara Marlowe, 'An Irishwoman's Diary': courtesy of *The Irish Times* • Philip Larkin, 'Letter to Monica Jones': Reproduced by kind permission of Faber and Faber Ltd • Joan Didion, 'Goodbye to all that' from *Slouching Towards Bethlehem*: Reprinted by permission of HarperCollins Publishers Ltd, © 1993, Joan Didion • George Orwell, *Why I Write*: (Copyright © George Orwell, 1933) by permission of Bill Hamilton as the Literary Executor of the Estate of the Late Sonia Brownell Orwell • Speech by Queen Elizabeth II: Used with permission under the (UK) Open Government Licence v2.0 • Speech by Mary Robinson: Used with permission of Mary Robinson • Philip French, 'Review of The Lives of Others': Copyright Guardian News and Media Ltd 2007 • Bernie Wright, 'Should Zoos be Closed?': © Bernie Wright, Alliance for Animal Rights • Veronica Chrisp: 'Should Zoos be Closed?': © Dublin Zoo • Brian Friel, *Dancing at Lughnasa*: Reproduced by kind permission of Faber and Faber Ltd • Dave Simpson, 'My Favourite Album': Copyright Guardian News and Media Ltd 2011 • Jonathan Jones 'The Meaning of 9/11's Most Controversial Photo': Copyright Guardian News and Media Ltd 2011 • Belinda McKeon, 'New York Stories on a Perfect Platform': Copyright © Belinda McKeon 2013. First published in The Irish Times and reproduced by permission of the author c/o Rogers, Coleridge & White Ltd., 20 Powis Mews, London, W11 1JN • CSO, *Women and Men in Ireland 2011*: Reproduced by permission from the Central Statistics Office, Ireland • Zadie Smith, 'Generation Why?': Copyright © Zadie Smith 2010. First published in *The New York Review of Books* and reproduced by permission of the author c/o Rogers, Coleridge & White Ltd., 20 Powis Mews, London, W11 1JN • Joseph Roth, What I Saw: Reproduced by permission of the author and Granta Books • GHOST TRAIN TO THE EASTERN STAR by Paul Theroux (2009): Reproduced with permission from Penguin Books • Dervla Murphy, 'First, Buy Your Pack Animal': Copyright Guardian News and Media Ltd 2009 • David Malouf, 'The Valley of the Lagoons': Copyright © David Malouf 2007. Reproduced by permission of the author c/o Rogers, Coleridge & White Ltd., 20 Powis Mews, London, W11 1JN • Claire Keegan, 'The Parting Gift': Reproduced with permission of Curtis Brown Group Ltd, London on behalf of Claire Keegan. Copyright © Claire Keegan 2007 • Hair by Chimamanda Ngozi Adichie. Copyright © Chimamanda Adichie, 2007, used by permission of The Wylie Agency (UK) Limited • 'Reunion' by John Cheever: From *Collected Stories* by John Cheever. Published by Vintage. Reprinted by permission of the Random House Group Limited • Gabriel García Márquez 'One of these Days': Gabriel García Márquez, "Un día de éstos", LOS FUNERALES DE LA MAMA GRANDE © Gabriel García Márquex, 1962 • 'One Of These Days' from NO ONE WRITES TO THE COLONEL AND OTHER STORIES by GABRIEL GARCIA MARQUEZ and TRANSLATED BY J.S. BERNSTEIN. Copyright © 1968 in the English translation by Harper & Row, Publishers, Inc. Reprinted by permission of HarperCollins Publishers

The publisher and author gratefully acknowledge the following for granting permission to reproduce photographs:
Clerys: By kind permission of the *Irish Independent* • Palimpsest cover: Little, Brown Book Group • *Just Kids* cover: © Patti Smith, 2011, *Just Kids*, Bloomsbury Publishing Plc • *The Speckled People* cover: Reprinted by permission of HarperCollins Publishers Ltd, © 2003, Hugo Hamilton • Cat and Neil Gaiman: Neil Gaiman, 2013 • Stephen Fry and NCFC: *Eastern Daily Press* • *A Woman in Berlin* (Anonymous) cover: Virago, an imprint of Little, Brown Book Group • Philip Larkin: The Society of Authors as the Literary Representative of the Estate of Philip Larkin (Hull History Centre: U DLV/2/5) • *Oxford Book of Essays* cover: By permission of Oxford University Press • Joan Didion: AP/Press Association Images • *Slouching Towards Bethlehem* cover: Reprinted by permission of HarperCollins Publishers Ltd, 1993, Joan Didion • Penguin Great Ideas: WHY I WRITE by George Orwell (Penguin Books, 2004). Cover reproduced with permission from Penguin Books • Queen Elizabeth II: Anwar Hussein/EMPICS Entertainment • Mary Robinson: Jennifer O'Gorman/July 2011/Dollow, Somalia • *Film Review 2012–2013* cover: Originally published by Titan Books • Berlin Wall: Time & Life Pictures/Getty Images • *Closer*, Joy Division, Factory album 1980, Photography by Bernard Pierre Wolff, Design Peter Saville with Martyn Atkins, Copyright Joy Division / Peter Saville • 9/11: By permission of Thomas Hoepker/Magnum Photos • Image 1: Getty Images • Image 2: Reproduced by permission Reuters/Mike Segar • Potsdamer Platz: Süddeutsche Zeitung Photo • *Blancanieves* poster: ©Arcadia Motion Pictures • Train: Copyright 2008, Seattle Times Company. Used with permission • Dervla Murphy: Copyright Dan Linehan • Dervla Murphy and bike: Copyright John Minihan • *Narratives and Narrators* cover: By permission of Oxford University Press • Oscar Wilde: Library of Congress • Image 1: THE WAVES by Virginia Woolf (Penguin Modern Classics, 2000). Cover reproduced with permission from Penguin Books • Image 2: ©1979, Virginia Woolf • *Walk to Blue Fields* cover: Reproduced by permission of Faber and Faber Ltd • Image 2, By permission of TopHam PicturePoint (Topfoto) • Paul's First Day: By courtesy of the Early Office Museum (officemuseum.com) • Alice Munro cover: AFP/Getty Images • *Canadian Short Stories* cover: Toronto Star via Getty Images • John Cheever: Getty Images • *Collected Stories* cover: Published by Vintage. Reprinted by permission of the Random House Group Limited • Gabriel Garcia Márquez: Jose Lara • Collected Stories cover: COLLECTED STORIES by Gabriel García Márquez (Penguin Books, 2008). Cover reproduced with permission from Penguin Books; all other photographs are from Glowimages • Alamy, Shutterstock and Wikicommons (public domain)

The author and publisher have made every effort to trace all copyright holders. If any have been overlooked we would be happy to make the necessary arrangements at the first opportunity.

Contents

How Excellence in English *works*

The aim of *Excellence in English* is to encourage students to develop a meaningful and sophisticated relationship with language.

Excellence in English is a **multimedia** concept. Students are provided with:

- A hard copy textbook
- An electronic version of the textbook
- Dedicated digital resources.

Icons are used throughout the textbook to indicate the availability of material on the website:

 Audio lecture

 Cloze test

 Worksheets

 Further material

The textbook is divided into three main sections:

1 Personal writing

2 Discursive writing

3 Narrative writing

Excellence in English examines language in all its complexity. While personal, discursive and narrative writing are explored as distinct genres, the textbook allows for the natural crossover and intersection of language. For example, while reading about the short story a student may learn to write a report.

Each section comprises four units: three for comprehension and one for composition. The Comprehending units prepare students to answer Question A and Question B tasks in Leaving Certificate Higher Level (HL) Paper 1 (Section I). The Composing units prepare students for the composition assignments set in Leaving Certificate HL Paper 1 (Section II).

Each **Comprehending** unit has an audio introduction and a cloze test PowerPoint slide to test students' understanding of key concepts. The units are modelled on a **READ–ANALYSE–MAKE** methodology, whereby students **read** texts, **analyse** texts and **make** texts themselves. Printable worksheets, incorporating a peer/self-evaluation, are available to accompany each 'make' task . Further material – texts, visuals, links – is also available on the website.

Each **Composing** unit has an audio introduction and other material – texts, visuals, links – available on the website. Again, students are provided with a graduated method of improving their composition skills. In each genre – personal essay, discursive essay and short story – students are invited to **read** and **analyse** texts before embarking on the **make** stage of composing texts themselves. Printable worksheets, incorporating a peer/self-evaluation, are available to accompany each 'make' task .

The book's **Introduction** answers five important questions:

1 What are the key ideas in the Leaving Certificate HL English syllabus?
2 What skills do I need in order to achieve well in Leaving Certificate HL English?
3 What will I be asked to do in the exam paper?
4 What is the best way to answer exam questions?
5 What is visual literacy?

Students should check in with the Introduction frequently as it contains the building blocks for success in Leaving Certificate HL Paper 1.

Finally, the **Help is at hand** section offers a useful guide to grammar, literary terms and vocabulary. **Literary terms** and more challenging words are colour coded throughout the textbook so that students can quickly and easily find the meaning of any vocabulary they do not understand.

Introduction

Syllabus: What are the key ideas in the Leaving Certificate English HL Paper 1 syllabus?

> This syllabus aims at initiating students into enriching experiences with language so that they become more adept and thoughtful users of it and more critically aware of its power and significance in their lives.
>
> Leaving Certificate HL English Syllabus

It is helpful to understand the key ideas behind the Leaving Certificate HL English Paper 1 syllabus. The syllabus is based on **genre theory** – an approach to teaching English that has grown out of the increasingly complex nature of language in the modern world. According to genre theory, everything is a text – an episode of *EastEnders*, a James Joyce short story, an advertisement on the back of a magazine.

The syllabus encourages you to engage with language in all its forms, to be curious as to how different texts are created and to model your own writing on that knowledge. This is known as **creative modelling**. Your task in Paper 1, therefore, is to encounter texts (**read**), to take them apart and see how they work (**analyse**), and then to create your own (**make**).

In the Comprehending section of Paper 1, Question A involves reading and analysing a text and Question B invites you to make a text. In the Composing section of Paper 1, your task is to make a composition. Each unit in *Excellence in English* is modelled on this **READ–ANALYSE–MAKE** methodology.

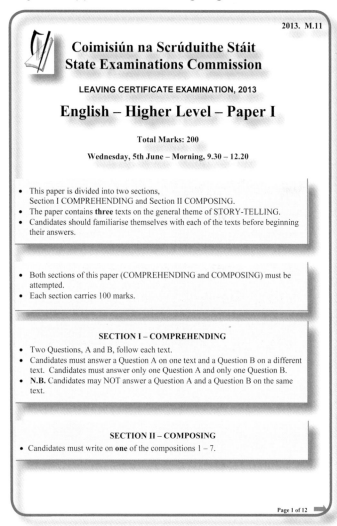

2013. M.11

Coimisiún na Scrúduithe Stáit
State Examinations Commission

LEAVING CERTIFICATE EXAMINATION, 2013

English – Higher Level – Paper I

Total Marks: 200

Wednesday, 5th June – Morning, 9.30 – 12.20

- This paper is divided into two sections,
  Section I COMPREHENDING and Section II COMPOSING.
- The paper contains **three** texts on the general theme of STORY-TELLING.
- Candidates should familiarise themselves with each of the texts before beginning their answers.

- Both sections of this paper (COMPREHENDING and COMPOSING) must be attempted.
- Each section carries 100 marks.

SECTION I – COMPREHENDING
- Two Questions, A and B, follow each text.
- Candidates must answer a Question A on one text and a Question B on a different text. Candidates must answer only one Question A and only one Question B.
- **N.B.** Candidates may NOT answer a Question A and a Question B on the same text.

SECTION II – COMPOSING
- Candidates must write on **one** of the compositions 1 – 7.

Page 1 of 12

1

Skills: What skills do I need to perform well in Leaving Certificate HL English Paper 1?

In the Leaving Certificate course, students will be encouraged to develop a more sophisticated range of skills and concepts. These will enable students to interpret, compose, discriminate and evaluate a range of material so that they become independent learners who can operate in the world beyond the school in a range of contexts.

Leaving Certificate HL English Syllabus

The skills required for success in Leaving Certificate HL English Paper 1 correspond closely to a learning model known as Bloom's Taxonomy, which was developed in the 1950s by Benjamin Bloom and modified by a group of cognitive psychologists in the 1990s. It sounds very complex, but it is not. Bloom is the name of the person who devised this idea and 'taxonomy' simply means to classify.

Bloom classified the different skills required for learning into six groups, all of which are needed in Leaving Certificate HL English Paper 1. The skills are graduated from one to six in terms of the level of thinking each requires. The exam paper reflects this gradation with questions ranging from the fairly straightforward to the more complex. In other words, the questions in Section I of the paper generally range from a comprehension question (What . . .) to a style question (How . . .).

It is helpful to understand the **verbs** associated with each skill, since they form the basis of questions on the paper:

1 **Remembering** or recalling is incredibly important for learning – it is the prior knowledge on which you build future learning.

   Verbs: define, list, recall, repeat, reproduce, state

2 **Understanding** something means that we can summarise information and use it in the future. This kind of thinking is useful for comprehension of texts.

   Verbs: explain, identify, locate, recognise, report, select, paraphrase

3 **Applying** is a very important skill. It means you can apply something you remember and understand to your own writing. This skill is essential in Question B tasks and in writing a composition.

   Verbs: choose, demonstrate, dramatise, employ, illustrate, interpret, sketch, use, write

4 **Analysing** something means to break it up into its component parts. Identifying stylistic features in a text on Paper 1 requires the skill of analysis.

   Verbs: appraise, compare, contrast, criticise, differentiate, distinguish, examine

2

5 **Evaluating** means to judge, assess or critique something. To do this you must have an idea of what qualities make a text successful. You may be asked to evaluate aspects of a text in Paper 1.

Verbs: appraise, argue, select, support, evaluate, compare, contrast

6 **Creating** is the most complex level of thinking. It means using what you know, understand, can apply, analyse and evaluate to create something completely new. This skill is required for Question B tasks and for writing a composition.

Verbs: assemble, construct, create, design, develop, formulate, write

Examination paper: What will I be asked to do?

Paper 1 is worth 200 marks, which is half the marks in Leaving Certificate English. It consists of two sections: Comprehending and Composing.

The **Comprehending** section contains three texts on a general theme that is printed on the front of the paper. You are advised to familiarise yourself with all texts before deciding which questions you wish to answer. You must answer two questions, one A and one B, from two different texts.

- **Question A** involves answering a series of questions on a particular text. It is worth 50 marks.

- **Question B** requires you to carry out a short writing assignment arising from a particular text. It is worth 50 marks.

The **Composing** section involves writing a composition on one of seven listed titles. It is worth 100 marks.

Recommended time allocation

Time management is essential in the exam. You must know your time allocation per question and stick to it.

You will have 2 hours and 50 minutes to complete Paper 1.
This may be broken down as follows:

Scanning through paper:	5 minutes
Question A:	50 minutes
Question B:	40 minutes
Composition:	70 minutes
Checking over paper:	5 minutes

INTRODUCTION

Marking criteria

It is also vital that you understand the marking scheme for English. Both Paper 1 and Paper 2 are marked according to this scheme.

30%	[P] Purpose	Engagement with the set task
30%	[C] Coherence	Sustaining response over the entire answer
30%	[L] Language	Appropriate to task – vocabulary, style, punctuation
10%	[M] Mechanics	Spelling, grammar

This marking scheme means:

[P] Answer the question you are asked.

[C] Stay focused on answering the question. Structure your answer properly.

[L] Express yourself fluently and clearly.

[M] Watch your spelling and grammar!

Examination questions: What is the best way to answer them?

Comprehending Question A guidelines

- Read the text. Examine the questions. Underline key words. Closely re-read the text with the questions in mind. Underline relevant sections of the text. Make notes on the exam paper. Only then should you begin to write out your answers.

- The marks can be distributed in a variety of ways so check the allocation of marks for each question. For every 5 marks, you should try to make at least one point with a relevant quotation or reference.

- Begin by explicitly answering the question. Each subsequent point should be made in a separate paragraph. Constantly refer back to the wording of the question in your answer. Finish with a brief conclusion.

- Give a detailed response including a quotation from or reference to the text to support your points.

- Remember, it is not enough to identify features of style. You must say what their function is in the context of the text you are analysing.

- Demonstrate mature evaluation. Treat the question in a critical manner where appropriate.

- Keep your writing style clear (use short sentences) and confident (precise and accurate expression).

Comprehending Question B guidelines

- Question B is a short writing assignment.

- Write one and a half to two pages.

- Plan your points and decide on a suitable form or layout.

- Think about your **register** – using language that is appropriate for the task. For example, the language used in a problem-page letter (casual, humorous, friendly) is different from the language used in a **speech** (formal, organised, logical, well informed).

- Apply yourself to the Question B task as though it were a real task. The more authentic your text is (content, layout, register and style) the better!

- Before you begin writing, ask yourself the following questions: Who are you writing as? Who are you writing for? What are you writing? What is the register? This will ensure that you cover all aspects of the question.

Composing guidelines

- You have a choice of seven titles, covering personal, discursive and **narrative** writing.

- A quotation from one of the three texts in the Comprehending section is used as a lead-in to each title. Remember, however, that this quotation is NOT the actual composition title, unless you are specifically instructed to use it as such. The composition title is printed in bold underneath the quotation.

- You may refer to the text from which the quotation is taken or you may complete the Composing assignment exclusively with reference to your own store of knowledge and experience. In fact, you are free to refer to, quote from or draw ideas from any or all of the texts and their accompanying illustrations. This is known as **creative modelling** and is very much encouraged in the new syllabus.

- When composing, there are three elements to consider: the **purpose** of the task, the **audience** for whom you are writing and the **register** appropriate to the task.

- While all **genres** interact and feed into each other, you must be clear about the workings of the particular composition you are writing: personal, discursive or narrative.

Visual literacy: What is it?

It is of primary importance in this syllabus that the students should engage with the domains of comprehending and composing in oral, written and, where possible, visual contexts.

Leaving Certificate HL English Syllabus

The **visual** is a hugely important dimension of our lives. It affects how we interpret the world, how we think of ourselves, how we dress and how we interact with our environment.

We live in a world saturated with visual images. Everywhere we look we are bombarded by billboard posters, TV, cinema, magazines, graphic novels, Facebook photographs and so on. And yet never before has the old adage 'the photograph never lies' been so untrue. In this age of digital manipulation, the photo may easily tell a lie. It is essential, therefore, to develop a critical eye when examining visual images, as well as the ability to recognise and understand ideas conveyed through visible images. The English syllabus recognises this, as visual literacy is examined in both the Comprehending section of Leaving Certificate Paper 1 and the study of film in the comparative study on Paper 2.

The texts in Paper 1 frequently contain a visual element – photos or pictures that accompany the written texts. You should be prepared to answer a visual literacy question. The key requirement is the ability to read an image. In order to do this you need to be aware that, when it comes to visuals, nothing is neutral, everything is suggestive.

Reading a visual text – key tips

- Spend some time examining the visual images before you begin to construct answers to the questions.

- Begin by identifying the main subject of the image. Focus then on the different areas or zones of the image: foreground, centre, background, left, right.

- Analyse carefully any props in the scene. What do they suggest?

- Remember, you are analysing the visual not just in terms of content, but also in terms of style. Note any striking or unusual details, any special effects such as camera angles, close-ups or blurring.

- Be aware of the importance of framing and light/dark/colour connotations. Remember, visual media communicate by suggestion.

- Look for linking or contrasting images and themes. Many photographs make use of **contrast**. One colour may be contrasted with another; shapes and textures may be contrasted. Photos often highlight the contrast between light and dark, movement and stillness, the human and the non-human.

- Determine the purpose of the visual and what it suggests to you. The word 'impact' refers to the effect the visual has on you, such as ideas, thoughts, aesthetic appreciation.

Reading a visual image – guide

Background – row of Christmas trees along upper floor of department store with strings of Christmas lights draped over them. In broad daylight the decorated trees fail to communicate in any magical or festive way.

The red 'Sale' signs in the window command the viewer's attention. Red is a powerful colour and attractive to the eye. It is also associated with Christmas. Figures on the poster – a woman and a boy – are presented in exaggerated guises. The woman has her head in her hand and exclaims in shock/disbelief. The boy holds a megaphone to his mouth.

The centre of the image is slightly out of focus, but is obviously a window display of perfume. The white and pink colours suggest glamour and femininity. The name of the department store is clearly seen across the top of all three windows. A classic black font on a pale blue background has connotations of longevity and tradition. The name of the store is also clearly visible on a small black plaque on a pillar, and on a black board above the grille. The gilded lettering suggests affluence.

Foreground – a large stretch of empty grey pavement. Remember, colour is never neutral – the grey footpath is drab.

The photo's subject matter is people waiting in order to be first into the department store for the post-Christmas sale. The image depicts three adults sitting on chairs with their backs to the camera. Their faces are obscured and their gender is not immediately obvious to a casual glance. The three people are strangely insignificant within the context of the image. Their huddled poses and wearing of hoods or hats lacks the excitement normally associated with shopping. The backdrop of a black grille endorses the low-key mood of the photo.

Overview: the photo communicates a tension between the marketing tactics employed by the store (suggesting power, glamour, wealth) and the small trio of figures sitting in the cold, waiting for the store to open. Remember, **contrast** creates tension in visual images.

Visual texts, including ones that you invent or recall, are generally described under the following headings:

Figures

- What figures are included in the image? Are they human, animal, fantastical or a combination of these?

- How are the figures presented? Are they in close-up, mid-shot or long shot (as small and inconsequential creatures)?

- How are the figures positioned within the **frame**? Do they dominate it from the centre or are they to one side? Are they entering or exiting?

INTRODUCTION

- How would you describe the body language of each figure? For example, alert, affectionate, fearful.
- How would you describe the facial expressions of each figure? For example, tense, relaxed, mournful.
- How do two or more figures within the frame relate to each other? For example, as lovers, as enemies, as colleagues.

Setting and objects

- What is the setting of the image? For example, a rural landscape, an urban scene, a wasteland.
- What objects are included in the image? These may be either as possessions of the figures or as background. Refer to realistic items and also to **symbols**.
- What text or design elements does the image contain? Are there words, geometric shapes, patterns and so on?

Colour and lighting

- Is the image in colour or is it black and white?
- If in colour, what colours are used? Which colour dominates? How do the colours relate to each other? What do they suggest?
- If in black and white, what lighting effects are used? For example, shafts of light, shadows, darkness.
- What other special effects are used? For example, camera angles, close-ups, blurring.

Personal

WRITING

 Memoir and autobiography

 Blog and interview

 Diary and letter

 Personal essay

Memoir and autobiography

Introduction

In this unit you will be introduced to two **genres** that embody the universal human desire to record experience: **memoir** and **autobiography**.

In his memoir, the American writer Gore Vidal offered a definition of the difference between memoir and autobiography. He said that a 'memoir is how one remembers one's own life, while an autobiography is history, requiring research, dates, facts double-checked'. Although there are no clear lines between the two genres, this is a pretty good definition of the differences between them.

Memoirs are structured differently from autobiographies, which often encompass the writer's entire life span. Memoirs tend to be about what can be learned from a section of one's life and often focus on the development of the author's personality.

Both memoir and autobiography offer some or all of the following features:

- An insight into the writer's personality.
- A reflective approach, offering interpretation, analysis and questions.
- An exploration of an inner life of feelings, emotions and ideas.
- The effective use of significant **anecdotes**, to provide drama, tension, humour and conflict.
- Descriptive writing capable of bringing a location to life on the page, since place is such an important influence on the formation of personality.
- Descriptive writing capable of bringing characters to life on the page, since people are such important influences on the formation of personality.
- Descriptive writing capable of bringing objects to life on the page, since objects are <u>formative</u> and significant influences.
- The <u>evocation</u> of atmosphere, using **imagery**, **sensory** detail, the weather and the seasons.

Biography is a detailed description or account of a person's life written by someone other than the subject. It entails more than basic facts (such as education, work, relationships, death). A biography also portrays a subject's experience of these events.

READ–ANALYSE–MAKE

In this text, which is adapted from the **memoir** *Just Kids* by the singer-songwriter, poet and visual artist Patti Smith, the writer describes her childhood and her early experiences of language and reading.

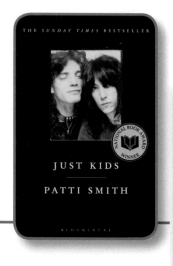

Personal WRITING

READ

from *Just Kids* by Patti Smith

When I was very young, my mother took me for walks in Humboldt Park, along the edge of the Prairie River. I have vague memories, like impressions on glass plates, of an old boathouse, a circular band shell, an arched stone bridge. The narrows of the river emptied into a wide lagoon and I saw upon its surface a singular miracle. A long curving neck rose from a dress of white plumage.

Swan, my mother said, sensing my excitement. It pattered the bright water, flapping its great wings, and lifted into the sky.

The word alone hardly attested to its magnificence nor conveyed the emotion it produced. The sight of it generated an urge I had no words for, a desire to speak of the swan, to say something of its whiteness, the explosive nature of its movement, and the slow beating of its wings.

The swan became one with the sky. I struggled to find words to describe my own sense of it. *Swan*, I repeated, not entirely satisfied, and I felt a twinge, a curious yearning, imperceptible to passersby, my mother, the trees, or the clouds.

I was born on a Monday, in the North Side of Chicago during the Great Blizzard of 1946. I came along a day too soon, as babies born on New Year's Eve left the hospital with a new refrigerator. Despite my mother's effort to hold me in, she went into heavy labor as the taxi crawled along Lake Michigan through a vortex of snow and wind. By my father's account, I arrived a long skinny thing with bronchial pneumonia, and he kept me alive by holding me over a steaming washtub.

My sister Linda followed during yet another blizzard in 1948. By necessity I was obliged to measure up quickly. My mother took in ironing as I sat on the stoop of our rooming house waiting for the iceman and the last of the horse-drawn wagons. He gave me slivers of ice wrapped in brown paper. I would slip one in my pocket for my baby sister, but when I later reached for it, I discovered it was gone.

When my mother became pregnant with my brother, Todd, we left our cramped quarters in Logan Square and migrated to Germantown, Pennsylvania. For the next few years we lived in temporary housing set up for servicemen and their children—whitewashed barracks overlooking an abandoned field alive with wildflowers. We called the field The Patch, and in summertime the grown-ups would sit and talk, smoke cigarettes, and pass around jars of dandelion wine while we children played. My mother taught us the games of her childhood: Statues, Red Rover, and Simon Says. We made daisy chains to adorn our necks and crown our heads. In the evenings we collected fireflies in mason jars, extracting their lights and making rings for our fingers.

My mother taught me to pray; she taught me the prayer her mother taught her. *Now I lay me down to sleep, I pray the Lord my soul to keep.* At nightfall, I knelt before my little bed as she stood, with her ever-present cigarette, listening as I recited after her. I wished nothing more than to say my prayers, yet these words troubled me and I plagued her with questions. What is the soul? What color is it? I suspected my soul, being mischievous, might slip away while I was dreaming and fail to return. I did my best not to fall asleep, to keep it inside of me where it belonged.

My love of prayer was gradually rivaled by my love for the book. I would sit at my mother's feet watching her drink coffee and smoke cigarettes with a book on her lap. Her absorption intrigued me. Though not yet in nursery school, I liked to look at her books, feel their paper, and lift the tissues from the frontispieces. I wanted to know what was in them, what captured her attention so deeply. When my mother discovered that I had hidden her crimson copy of Foxe's *Book of Martyrs* beneath my pillow, with hopes of absorbing its meaning, she sat me down and began the laborious process of teaching me to read. With great effort we moved through Mother Goose to Dr. Seuss. When I advanced past the need for instruction, I was permitted to join her on our overstuffed sofa, she reading *The Shoes of the Fisherman* and I *The Red Shoes*.

I was completely smitten by the book. I longed to read them all, and the things I read of produced new yearnings. Perhaps I might go off to Africa and offer my services to Albert Schweitzer or, decked in my coonskin cap and powder horn, I might defend the people like Davy Crockett. I could scale the Himalayas and live in a cave spinning a prayer wheel, keeping the earth turning. But the urge to express myself was my strongest desire, and my siblings were my first eager coconspirators in the harvesting of my imagination. They listened attentively to my stories, willingly performed in my plays, and fought valiantly in my wars. With them in my corner, anything seemed possible.

Written text

The opening of the text is perfectly suited to the **genre** of **memoir**. It is a personal **anecdote** relating to an early childhood memory and evoking a significant personal experience.

A striking **simile** – 'like impressions on glass plates' – draws the reader's attention to the **subjective** nature of memory. It is this kind of subjective reflection that marks out the better texts in this genre. Detail is used to create **imagery** ('an old boat house, a circular band shell, an arched stone bridge') and a beautiful description of a swan is presented from the **point of view** of a young child: 'A long curving neck rose from a dress of white plumage.' The wonder of the child's early engagement with language is captured in the mother's naming of the 'miracle' vision as a swan. Carefully selected **verbs** keep the action alive: the river 'emptied', the swan 'pattered'. The inadequacy of a single word to express fully all that the child experiences is beautifully captured, and provides thoughtful musing by Smith on the nature of language itself.

The text extends from the opening anecdote into **reportage** at paragraph five. Good memoir is a meshing of the private and public aspects of life. The reader is offered a brief account of Smith's family history, including the births of her siblings and where the family lived. Woven into this account is further casual musing about the nature of life. The child learns that nothing lasts, nothing stays the same. The slivers of ice that she puts in her pocket melt and disappear.

Smith captures the world of her childhood in powerful sense impressions. We feel the 'cramped quarters', we see the 'whitewashed barracks', we smell the wildflowers and the cigarettes. The naming of the games the children played – 'Statues, Red Rover, and Simon Says' – and the detailed account of extracting the firefly light enrich the text with **realism**.

The child's initiation into the world of prayer alerts her to the complexity of language. **Rhetorical questions** are used effectively to illustrate the drama taking place within the child's mind, a drama that ultimately finds expression in reading.

The extract began with the young child's introduction to words and ends with Smith recounting her childhood love of books: 'I was completely smitten by the book.' This structure gives the extract a unifying theme: language. The journey from books out into the world of the imagination and into the creation of her own stories is a wonderful culmination to this opening extract from Smith's memoir.

Visual text

In 1975 Arista Records released *Horses*, the first rock album by New York bohemian poet Patti Smith. The stark cover photograph, taken by Robert Mapplethorpe, was devastatingly original. The critic Camille Paglia describes it as the most electrifying image she had ever seen of a woman of her generation. Mapplethorpe's portrait symbolised women's new liberation in the 1970s. Before Patti Smith, women in rock music had presented themselves in conventional roles such as folk singers or motorcycle chicks. As this photo shows, Smith's <u>persona</u> was brand-new.

Patti Smith Horses

Smith was the first to claim an identity outside the traditional understanding of gender roles. Rumpled and unkempt, she defies the conventional rules of femininity. Her gaze into the lens of the camera is unflinching, her pose masculine and assertive, her clothes deliberately <u>androgynous</u>. No female rocker had ever dominated an image in such an aggressive and uncompromising way.

Shot in high-**contrast** black and white, Mapplethorpe's photo unites the style of European art films with that of glamorous, high-fashion magazines.

Personal WRITING

MAKE

QUESTION B

You have been asked to give **a short talk on radio** about a place that is important to you. Write out the text of the talk you would give. (50)

Sample answer

You are listening to the *Nancy Moore Show* on KYL Radio, where it's time for 'People and Places'. This week the writer Miriam Lloyd talks about the place that is important to her.

Over to you, Miriam . . .

Connemara in the West of Ireland is an important place to me. It is my place of escape, my retreat from the world. Many people have a special place in their heart that offers comfort and refuge from the stresses and strains of life. I think of poets like W. B. Yeats and his desire to leave 'pavements grey' and go to the island of Innisfree, or William Wordsworth and his great love for nature which he saw as an escape from 'the din of towns and cities'. I go to Connemara as often as I can and when I leave it again I am restored and rested.

The landscape of Connemara is unique. Writers and artists from all parts of the world have praised its beauty. Close your eyes and imagine the rugged outcrop of rock and mountain, the rolling waves of the Atlantic Ocean, the call of wild birds echoing out over untouched terrain. This is Connemara – a wild and free area of Ireland where the pace of life is slow and the rest of the world is far away.

And yet that is not all there is to Connemara. The area is renowned for excellent hospitality. After a long solitary walk over bog land and beach there is nothing I enjoy more than a good chowder in a local bar and a chat with friendly locals. Connemara is full of excellent restaurants, cafés and pubs; perfect places to while away a few hours reading a book by an open fire in winter or lost in the timeless contemplation of your own thoughts.

Finally, listeners, let me share a particular image with you. An image that I stir up from the cauldron of memory whenever I need some comfort or beauty in my life. It is evening and the gloaming is casting its spell on the Sky Road just outside Clifden. As I walk I am buffeted by a clear and salty wind. On one side of me mountains rise up into the air, on the other side the sea crashes against the shore. All around me is the glory of untouched nature.

Cut to music – Vivaldi's 'Four Seasons'.

Techniques: Radio talk

- Choose a **register** to complement your approach to the task (such as formal, relaxed, humorous).
- Invent the name of the radio station.
- Mention the name of the radio programme. If you wish, you may also take over from or hand back to another presenter.

- Help your audience absorb information by providing them with images and by using rhetorical devices.
- Remember that your audience cannot see you, so you need to transport them to a three-dimensional world by using **sensory imagery**.

Over to you: Read and analyse

As you read the following text from the 2012 Leaving Certificate exam paper, take note of the annotations in the margins and see if you can isolate the particular words and phrases that the annotations refer to. In this way you will improve your skills in both reading and analysing.

Text 1, 2012: Personal memories

This edited extract is adapted from *Where the World Began* by Canadian writer Margaret Laurence, in which she remembers and reflects on the small prairie town where she grew up.

Mystery of place captured in opening paragraph
Compound word

A strange place it was, that place where the world began. A place of incredible happenings, splendours and revelations, despairs like multitudinous pits of isolated hells. A place of shadow-spookiness, inhabited by the unknowable dead. A place of jubilation and of mourning, horrible and beautiful.

Contrast used for dramatic effect

Factual statement

It was, in fact, a small prairie town.

Personal tone

Because that settlement and that land were my first and for many years my only real knowledge of this planet, in some profound way they remain my world, my way of viewing. My eyes were formed there. Towns like ours, set in a sea of land, have been described thousands of times as dull, bleak, flat, uninteresting. All I can say is – well, you really have to live there to know that country. The town of my childhood could be called bizarre, agonizingly repressive or cruel at times, and the land in which it grew could be called harsh in the violence of its seasonal changes. But never merely flat or uninteresting. Never dull.

Forceful language to emphasise point

Long sentences used to create reflective tone

Addresses reader

Repetition for effect

Anecdote

In winter, we used to hitch rides on the back of the milk sleigh, our moccasins squeaking and slithering on the hard rutted snow of the roads, our hands in ice-bubbled mitts hanging onto the box edge of the sleigh for dear life. Those mornings, rising, there would be the perpetual fascination of the frost feathers on windows, the ferns and flowers and eerie faces traced there during the night by unseen

Detail used to bring account to life

Powerful visual imagery

Use of **simile**

Interesting use of **verbs**

Striking use of **metaphor**

Description enhanced by use of **alliteration**

Use of **onomatopoeia**

Poetic use of **sibilance**

Concrete illustration used to support point

Further use of examples

Prolepsis creates a reflective tone

Use of **metaphor**

Glimpse into way of life of the town

Use of second person **point of view** to draw reader into the text

Auditory imagery brings the text to life

Hyperbole used for effect

Colloquial language adds authenticity to the text

Use of **olfactory** image

Detail brings the text to life

Insight into author at eighteen

Long sentences enhance the reflective tone

artists of the wind. Evenings, coming back from skating, the sky would be black but not dark, for you could see a cold glitter of stars from one side of the earth's rim to the other. And then the sometime astonishment when you saw the Northern Lights flaring across the sky, like the scrawled signature of God. After a blizzard, when the snowploughs hadn't yet got through, school would be closed for the day, the assumption being that the town's young could not possibly flounder through five feet of snow in the pursuit of education.

We would then gaily don snowshoes and flounder for miles out into the white dazzling deserts, in pursuit of a different kind of knowing. If you came back too close to night, through the woods at the foot of the town hill, the thin black branches of poplar and chokecherry now meringued with frost, sometimes you heard coyotes. Or maybe the banshee wolf-voices were really only inside your head.

Summers were scorching, and when no rain came and the wheat became bleached and dried before it headed, the faces of farmers and townsfolk would not smile much. Yet the outside world had its continuing marvels. The poplar bluffs and the small river were filled and surrounded with a zillion different grasses, stones, and weed flowers. The meadowlarks sang undaunted from the twanging telephone wires along the gravel highway. Once we found an old flat-bottomed scow (boat), and launched her, poling along the shallow brown waters, mending her with wodges of hastily chewed Spearmint, grounding her among the tangles of yellow marsh marigolds that grew succulently along the banks of the shrunken river, while the sun made our skins smell dusty-warm.

The oddities of the place were endless. An elderly lady used to serve, as her afternoon tea offering to other ladies, soda biscuits spread with peanut butter and topped with a whole marshmallow. Some considered this slightly eccentric, when compared with chopped egg sandwiches, and admittedly talked about her behind her back, but no one ever refused these delicacies. Another lady dyed her hair a bright and cheery orange, by strangers often mistaken at twenty paces for a feather hat. My own beloved stepmother wore a silver fox neckpiece, a whole pelt, with the embalmed head still on.

When I was eighteen, I couldn't wait to get out of that town, away from the prairies. I did not know then that I would carry the land and town all my life within my skull, and they would form the mainspring and source of the writing I was to do, wherever and however far away I might live.

This was my territory in the time of my youth, and in a sense my life since then has been an attempt to look at it, to come to terms with it. Stultifying to the mind it certainly could be, and sometimes was, but not to the imagination. It was many things, but it was never dull.

Repetition of keywords echoes the beginning of the text, giving the text a unifying strand of thought

My true roots were here. This is where my world began. A world which formed me, and continues to do so, even while I fought it in some of its aspects, and continue to do so. A world which gave me my own lifework to do, because it was here that I learned the sight of my own particular eyes.

Resolution is strongly personal and shorter sentences add a tone of certainty to the final musings

Answer the following Leaving Certificate questions using the guidelines below.

QUESTION A

(i) Margaret Laurence claims that the world of her childhood was 'never dull'. In your opinion, which **three** pieces of evidence from the text most effectively support her claim? In each case, briefly explain your choice. (15)

(ii) What do the last three paragraphs reveal about the writer's present attitude to the small prairie town where she grew up? (15)

(iii) Do you think this passage is a good example of effective autobiographical writing? Give reasons for your answer. (20)

Answer guidelines

Part (i): begin by explicitly answering the question; for instance, *Margaret Laurence claims that the world of her childhood was 'never dull' and offers evidence to support her claim*. Then select the three pieces of evidence from the text that you think most effectively support her claim. Possible points include: enthusiastic opening description; natural world's 'continuing marvels'; freedom of childhood, outdoor activities; the endless 'oddities of the place'.

Part (ii): begin by answering the question; for instance, *The last three paragraphs reveal much about the writer's present attitude to the small prairie town where she grew up*. Then isolate at least three aspects of the writer's attitude from these paragraphs and examine each in turn. Possible points include: changed perspective on the impact of the small prairie town; keen awareness of the town as a 'source' of her writing; realistic and balanced viewpoint of past experiences; personal and definitive tone of appreciation.

Part (iii): this question invites you to examine the style of the text – how it is written. Begin by answering the question; for instance, *I think this passage is an excellent example of autobiographical writing*. Then select techniques used by the writer, explaining how they enhance the telling of her personal story. Possible points include: reflective, personal voice; interesting **anecdotal** details of childhood; engaging atmosphere, authentic sense of place; descriptive language, evocative **imagery**.

Personal WRITING

Over to you: Make

Answer the following Leaving Certificate question using the tips and techniques below.

QUESTION B

Write **a letter** to Margaret Laurence, in response to Text 1, commenting on what you find interesting in the extract, and telling her about your home place and its <u>impact</u> on you. (50)

Answer tips

You will be rewarded for the following:

- Clear appreciation of the task
- Consistency of **register**
- Effective use of reference
- Quality of your writing.

Techniques: Letter

Personal

- Put your address and the date in the top right-hand corner.
- Begin and end in a friendly way.
- Organise your letter into paragraphs.

Formal

- Put your address and the date in the top right-hand corner.
- Put the recipient's address on the left side of the page, below your address and the date.
- If you do not know the person's name, start with either 'To whom it may concern' or 'Dear Sir/Madam'.
- Organise your letter into paragraphs.
- End with 'Yours sincerely' if you know the person and 'Yours faithfully' if you don't.

To an editor

- Start with 'Sir' or 'Madam' and end with 'Yours etc.'
- Put your name and address at the end.

Test yourself

In this text, adapted from the memoir *The Speckled People* by the Irish writer Hugo Hamilton, the author captures the bewilderment of his early childhood, when little in the world seemed to make sense to a boy whose father was Irish and whose mother was German.

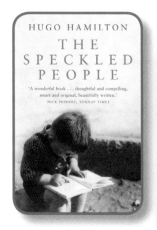

from *The Speckled People* by Hugo Hamilton

When you're small you know nothing.

When I was small I woke up in Germany. I heard the bells and rubbed my eyes and saw the wind pushing the curtains like a big belly. Then I got up and looked out the window and saw Ireland. And after breakfast we all went out the door to Ireland and walked down to Mass. And after Mass we walked down to the big green park in front of the sea because I wanted to show my mother and father how I could stand on the ball for a count of three, until the ball squirted away from under my feet. I chased after it, but I could see nothing with the sun in my eyes and I fell over a man lying on the grass with his mouth open. He sat up suddenly and said, 'What the Jayses?' He told me to look where I was going in future. So I got up quickly and ran back to my mother and father. I told them that the man said 'Jayses', but they were both turned away, laughing at the sea. My father was laughing and blinking through his glasses and my mother had her hand over her mouth, laughing and laughing at the sea, until the tears came into her eyes and I thought, maybe she's not laughing at all but crying.

How do you know what that means when her shoulders are shaking and her eyes are red and she can't talk? How do you know if she's happy or sad? And how do you know if your father is happy or whether he's still angry at all the things that are not finished yet in Ireland. You know the sky is blue and the sea is blue and they meet somewhere, far away at the horizon. You can see the white sailing boats stuck on the water and the people walking along with ice-cream cones. You can hear a dog barking at the waves. You can see him standing in the water, barking and trying to bite the foam. You can see how long it takes for the sound of the barking to come across, as if it's coming from somewhere else and doesn't belong to the dog at all any more, as if he's barking and barking so much that he's hoarse and lost his voice.

When you're small you know nothing. You don't know where you are, or who you are, or what questions to ask.

Then one day my mother and father did a funny thing. First of all, my mother sent a letter home to Germany and asked one of her sisters to send over new trousers for my brother and me. She wanted us to wear something German – lederhosen. When the parcel arrived, we couldn't wait to put them on

Personal WRITING

and run outside, all the way down the lane at the back of the houses. My mother couldn't believe her eyes. She stood back and clapped her hands together and said we were real boys now. No matter how much we climbed on walls or trees, she said, these German leather trousers were indestructible, and so they were. Then my father wanted us to wear something Irish too. He went straight out and bought hand-knit Aran sweaters. Big, white, rope patterned, woollen sweaters from the west of Ireland that were also indestructible. So my brother and I ran out wearing lederhosen and Aran sweaters, smelling of rough wool and new leather, Irish on top and German below. We were indestructible. We could slide down granite rocks. We could fall on nails and sit on glass. Nothing could sting us now and we ran down the lane faster than ever before, brushing past nettles as high as our shoulders.

When you're small you're like a piece of white paper with nothing written on it. My father writes down his name in Irish and my mother writes down her name in German and there's a blank space left over for all the people outside who speak English. We're special because we speak Irish and German and we like the smell of these new clothes. My mother says it's like being at home again and my father says your language is your home and your country is your language and your language is your flag.

But you don't want to be special. Out there in Ireland you want to be the same as everyone else, not an Irish speaker, not a German or a Kraut or a Nazi. On the way down to the shops, they call us the Nazi brothers. They say we're guilty and I go home and tell my mother I did nothing. But she shakes her head and says I can't say that. I can't deny anything and I can't fight back and I can't say I'm innocent. She says it's not important to win. Instead, she teaches us to surrender, to walk straight by and ignore them.

QUESTION A

(i)   Based on your reading of the above text, what impression do you form of the writer, Hugo Hamilton, as a boy? Support your view with reference to the text. (15)

(ii) Based on your reading of this extract, suggest three appropriate images you could use to illustrate this text. Briefly explain your selection in all three cases. (15)

(iii) Do you think this passage is a good example of effective autobiographical writing? Give reasons for your answer. (20)

QUESTION B

'She says it's not important to win.'

Write the text for a short radio talk where you explain the importance, or unimportance, of winning for you.

Blog and interview

Introduction

In this unit you will be introduced to two **genres** that have their origins in conversation: the blog and the interview.

A **blog** is a discussion or informational site published on the world wide web and consisting of discrete entries, known as 'posts', typically displayed in reverse order – the most recent post appears first. It is easy to appreciate how blogs can be seen as a modern form of letter writing – the verb 'posted' is used to indicate that a blog entry has been uploaded.

The word 'blog' is a contraction of the words 'web log'. Blog can also be used as a **verb**, meaning to maintain a blog. While many blogs provide commentary on a particular subject, others function more as personal online diaries. Indeed, the modern blog evolved from the online **diary**, where people kept a running account of their personal lives. Some blogs function as online brand advertising.

Blogs are usually the work of a single individual and often cover a single subject. Multi-author blogs (MABs), with posts that are written by a large number of different authors and that are professionally edited, are a more recent development. MABs from newspapers, other media outlets, universities and interest groups account for an increasing quantity of blog traffic.

A typical blog combines text, images and links to other blogs, web pages and media related to its topic. The majority of blogs are interactive, allowing visitors to leave comments and even send messages to each other, and it is this interactivity that distinguishes them from other static websites. In that sense, blogging can be seen as a form of social networking. The rise of Twitter and other 'microblogging' systems has contributed to the huge growth of blogs in recent years.

A standard feature of many contemporary blogs is the **interview**, in which the blogger interviews successful or well-known personalities as a means of boosting traffic to their own blog. An interview is a conversation between two or more people during which questions are asked by the interviewer to elicit facts or statements from the interviewee. Interviews are a standard part of traditional journalism, as well as of blogs.

The key features common to both the blog and the interview are an immediate and conversational tone, and a relaxed, informal **register**.

READ–ANALYSE–MAKE

In this text, which is adapted from the blog he maintains on his website, writer Neil Gaiman, author of the comic book series *The Sandman* and novels *Stardust*, *Coraline* and *The Graveyard Book*, describes his day-to-day life.

'Princess, and Some Thoughts on Writing' by Neil Gaiman

SATURDAY, MARCH 30, 2013

Princess, and some thoughts on writing

POSTED BY NEIL GAIMAN AT 9:34 AM

Princess, my old, old old cat, is coming to the end of her life. She's somewhere over 20, but we do not know how much over 20 she is, as she was living wild in the woods for at least a year before she decided to live in our house instead. Right now she's in the bathroom in the attic, beside the space heater, sleeping most of the time.

This is her on my lap last night.

Because she is in the attic I went into the attic last night, and while I was there I looked in some tubs of papers. I found one marked Poems, and found myself flicking through sheafs of discolouring papers with poems or drawings or prose on them, including the first ever description of Mr Croup and Mr Vandemar by Neil Gaiman aged 17 (only I spelled it Kroop then), with a drawing of each of them.

And what amazed me was that there was almost nothing there that was written by *me*. I'd sound like e.e.cummings one moment and an awkward mash-up of Moorcock and Zelazny the next. You can tell exactly when I've been reading the complete poems of Rudyard Kipling . . . I could point to every poem, every unfinished fragment of prose in that folder, and tell you who I'd been reading, what I was thinking at the time. *Everything* read like a bad imitation of somebody else. There wasn't anything in there that indicated that I was going to be a writer, a real writer, with something to say, except for one thing, and it was this:

I was writing. There was lots of writing going on.

And that made up for so much. I never knew how to finish anything longer than a couple of pages, but I was writing.

When SHARED WORLDS asked me (and other writers) to write some writing advice on our hands (it's at http://www.wofford.edu/sharedworlds/handinhand.aspx – go and look), I wrote this:

You want to be a writer?

Keep writing.

Personal WRITING

Written text

ANALYSE

The **blog** opens in a casual, conversational way. An intimate tone is established with the online reader: 'Princess, my old, old old cat, is coming to the end of her life.' Short sentences make the blog easy to read, as does the use of some single-line paragraphs. Other attributes of blogs that can be seen in this text include links, brackets, *italics*, **ellipsis** and questions.

There is an interdependence between written and visual texts. Gaiman tells us about his cat in simple language and then draws our attention to a photograph of her: 'This is her on my lap last night.' He makes connections between his cat and writing by simple associations: cat, attic, old papers, thoughts on writing. The human mind naturally works this way and so an author wandering easily from subject to subject is a common characteristic of blogs.

Gaiman makes a lot of **allusions** in the blog. He mentions Mr Croup and Mr Vandemar, who are two characters from his television series *Neverland*. He also refers to the poet e.e. cummings, and the science fiction writers Moorcock and Zelazny. This is a feature of blogs. Because the reader is generally a fan of the writer, there is a shared cultural vocabulary between them, and therefore a reasonable assumption on the part of the writer that the reader will understand such allusions.

Gaiman makes some interesting observations about writing. He refers to the papers in the attic by 'Neil Gaiman aged 17' and is amazed that 'there was almost nothing there that was written by me'. He admits that his early work was imitative and asserts that a person becomes a writer by consistently writing. The blog concludes with Gaiman telling (and showing) us the advice about writing he wrote on his hand in response to a request from Shared Worlds, a creative writing programme for teenagers.

Personal WRITING

Visual text

The first image is a photograph of Gaiman's cat, Princess. The photograph has an amateur quality – there is some blurring – which adds to its charm. Princess is positioned on Gaiman's lap. Gaiman is sitting, almost in silhouette, at the left edge of the frame. The contrast between the white of the cat and the black of Gaiman's clothes is striking.

The second image is a photograph of Gaiman displaying advice that he has written on the palm of his hand. It was taken with the purpose of being displayed on the Shared Worlds website and is, therefore, more professional in appearance. The location of the photograph appears to be Gaiman's study. In the background there is wood panelling to the right and a desk on the left with objects on it: a box, a plant and some curious ornaments, including a Dalek from *Dr Who* and a Groucho Marx figurine. Behind the desk is a window through which a garden is visible. Gaiman is positioned pretty much in the centre of the frame. He is wearing a dark jumper (dark clothes are synonymous with Neil Gaiman). His hand is in front of his face and on his palm is written – 'Write. Finish Things. Keep Writing'. Gaiman's right eye, peeping from behind his hand, looks out directly into the viewer's gaze.

QUESTION B

Imagine you have been asked to write **a blog** on a tourism website promoting Ireland's artistic and cultural attractions (literature, art, music, etc.). Write the text of the blog. (50)

MAKE

Sample answer

http://tourismireland.ie/blogs/Arts/

Home

Galleries

Upcoming events

Hotels / B&Bs

Blogs

Contact

Come one, come all. Feast on the treats the Emerald Isle has to offer. I have spent the last week happily trudging from county to county to find the best tourist attractions in Ireland!

As soon as you step outside your hotel, you will find yourself enthralled by the variety of artistic and cultural attractions Ireland has to offer. Whether you are looking for somewhere to take the kids on a Saturday afternoon or you've flown thousands of miles to get the true 'Éire' experience, there is something out there for you.

If you are strolling through Dublin's cobbled streets and listening to traditional music blasting out from pub doors, then you are probably in Temple Bar. Temple Bar is arguably the cultural hub of the city and if you're interested in seeing a 'rare auld' céilí band in full swing, then this is your stop.

If your taste is modern – less fiddle, more funk – then Punchestown in County Kildare is the place for you. In summer the racecourse venue plays host to one of Europe's most popular music festivals, <u>Oxegen</u>, so pack your wellies and your tent, and you'll be 'sucking diesel' (Irish expression for going well).

Those of you who are art lovers will not believe your eyes when you visit Ireland. Forget conventional 'done-to-death' old art and find a new passion on the streets of Dublin, Cork or Limerick. It seems like up-and-coming artists are selling their wares on every corner. Stop and take a gander – you might just discover the new Picasso!

If paintings and pictures are not your thing, then feast your eyes at the <u>Wax Museum</u>, just off Dame Street in Dublin. This little gem lets you walk around, touch and take photos with art.

One cannot write about the arts in Ireland without mentioning literature. Some of the best writers in the world hail from Irish soil. Beckett, Yeats, Joyce. So, 'arise and go now . . .' Annual festivals from Bantry to Belfast celebrate all things literary. Plays are performed, poems read, speeches recited. A must for any budding writer.

In short, Ireland has more to offer than could ever be squeezed into a blog. For a full list of upcoming events see <u>Ireland Event Guide</u>.

Visit Kilkenny Castle – the home of medieval Ireland
Advertisement for Wax Museum

Techniques: Blog

- Design your text so that it looks somewhat like a blog. Remember, layout is important.
- Adopt a conversational tone.
- Maintain a chatty, informal **register**.
- Comply with the demands of the question – in the case above, to promote Ireland's artistic and cultural attractions.
- Offer specific examples rather than generalisations.

Over to you: Read and analyse

As you read the following text from the 2010 Leaving Certificate exam paper, take note of the annotations in the margins and see if you can isolate the particular words and phrases that the annotations refer to. In this way you will improve your skills in both reading and analysing.

Text 1, 2010: A personal future

This text is a short extract adapted from *Stepping Stones: Interviews with Seamus Heaney* by Dennis O'Driscoll in which Heaney reflects on the impact of his childhood on his future life as a poet.

The opening question both provides and elicits information

Was there any real prospect that – as the eldest son – you might follow in your father's footsteps as farmer or cattle dealer?

Inverted commas highlight that a word is being used in a particular context

Once I went to secondary school I suppose there was the presumption all round that whatever I did at the end of my time there, I wouldn't be back on the farm. I was being "educated", and that meant being set apart. In spite of enjoying work on the farm during the summer, I never had a desire to get involved in any serious way in cattle dealing. I was familiar with the environs of fair hills and cattle pens and I knew men in the trade and enjoyed the banter and the bidding and bargaining, slapping hands, throwing up the hands, walking away, pretending you were at your limit – it was terrific theatre and I didn't feel out of it; but I still didn't have an ambition to grow up and do it.

Personal tone established through repeated use of 'I'

Verbs bring the action of the cattle market to life

Alliteration and use of triadic structure add to description

Use of metaphor

Question invites Heaney to discuss his relationship with his father

How did your father feel about the educational path you chose as your future?

There was a strong streak of fatalism in my father. For a start, he didn't talk much about our future – or about anything: the notion that there were options, that a future could be projected, that a change might be effected, I don't think he took that in. He was out on the road, earning a living. He would have regarded himself as more lord than labourer. There was a touch of the artist about him, I suppose. A certain pride, a certain freedom that came from being on the road, among the cattle people. He would have seen himself endowed with a definite position because of that, different from the neighbours who just farmed the land. To put it another way, he would have seen dealing as a calling and would have known that I hadn't been called.

Variety of sentence lengths

Colloquial expression creates intimacy between interviewer and interviewee

Colloquial expression reflects the oral nature of the text

Use of alliteration to make a phrase memorable

Detailed drawing out of point

Question is designed to gain insight into Heaney as a student

Were you the kind of pupil whose essays were held up by the teacher as a shining example to the rest of the class?

I remember a moment early in my secondary schooling when we were asked to write on the topic "A Day at the Seaside". In the middle of the list of usual, expected activities such as diving and swimming, neither of which I could do, I wrote about going into an amusement arcade to escape from a shower and being depressed by the wet footprints on the floor and the cold, wet atmosphere created by people in their rained-on summer clothes. This had actually happened to me, so the image and recording of it had a different feel. Something in me knew that I was on the right track – but it took me years to follow up, the writer-in-waiting if you like. Early-in-life experience has been central to me. It's like a culture at the bottom of a jar, although it doesn't grow, I think, or help anything else to grow, unless you find a way to reach it and touch it. But once you do, it's like putting your hand into a nest and finding something beginning to hatch out in your head.

Personal anecdote used to illustrate experience of school; reveals Heaney's original vision, even at a young age

Repetition of 'wet' expresses mood of essay

Important disclosure – importance of formative years

Effective use of simile

Effective use of metaphor

Use of second person invites the interviewer to relate to point being made

Specific question from interviewer

A blind musician, Rosie Keenan, is mentioned in your poetry. What made this neighbour so special to you?

Analogy adds clarity

The blindness itself was the wonder. The Keenans lived only a couple of fields away from us, in the country equivalent of 'the next block'. Rosie would often be out on the road, sometimes on her own, sometimes with her sister. This was the Broagh Road, a side road, and in those days the traffic amounted to no more than a few locals on bicycles and the occasional horse and cart, so she was safe enough, walking tall and straight, her white stick in her hand, her pale face looking straight ahead, unwavering and unseeing. She came home for the school holidays – she worked in Belfast, in some capacity in a school for the blind. When I first knew her she would have been in her late thirties or early forties, a contemporary of my mother's, who had been in school with her. So there was great ease between them and always a sweet atmosphere when she came to the house.

Concrete details (names of people and places) add to honest nature of the exchange

*Detail allows for vivid **characterisation***

Background detail adds to character sketch

Relationship between the women captured in a single phrase

Question designed to elicit information about family dynamics

Were you and your siblings pressed into service as her guides?

We were not. The pressure was to perform for her, to sing a school song or say a school poem. She would often bring her violin because my mother loved her to play and sing: Irish dance tunes mostly, jigs and reels, Thomas Moore songs. So her visit would turn into a little home concert. She made that musical dimension a living thing for us. She also had a piano at home and, in the middle of the day, we'd often hear her playing as we passed by Keenans' house – which I always found strange, because in our experience the daytime was when grown-ups were out working. But as the years have gone by, I've begun to think of her as the one who first made time and space in our lives for art. Our blind Rosie, like Blind Raftery – 'playing music to empty pockets'.

Response to question is emphatic

Descriptive detail is used to bring the scene to life

*Effective use of **auditory imagery***

Text finishes on a reflective note

Pithy quotation is apt and memorable

Answer the following Leaving Certificate questions using the guidelines below.

QUESTION A

(i) It has been said that a strong sense of the place and community in which Heaney grew up emerges from this interview. Do you agree? Support your view with reference to the text. (15)

(ii) Based on your reading of this extract, suggest **three** appropriate images you could use to illustrate this text. Briefly explain your selection in all three cases. (15)

(iii) What impression of Seamus Heaney do you form from reading this interview? Refer to the text (content and style) in support of your answer. (20)

Answer guidelines

Part (i): begin by explicitly answering the question; for instance, *I agree that a strong sense of the place and community in which Heaney grew up emerges from this interview.* Remember

Personal WRITING

that you are free to agree or disagree with the idea that a sense of place and community emerges from the interview. Possible points include: quiet rural setting and familiar places; 'environs of fair hills'; lively banter and bargaining of the cattle people; seaside trip, neighbour's visit or home concert.

Part (ii): begin by answering the question; for instance, *Based on my reading of this extract, I have selected three images that would appropriately illustrate it.* Focus your answer on three specific images. Offer a clear description of each image **and** an explanation as to how each image illustrates/complements the text.

Part (iii): this question invites you to examine the style of the text – how it is written. Begin by answering the question; for instance, *From reading the interview I form a strong impression of Seamus Heaney.* Focus clearly on aspects of Heaney's personality/character by referring to both content and style, though not necessarily equally. Possible points include: lively, open personality echoed in ideas and tone; keen observer of people and places evident in descriptive detail; unpretentious, unaffected by success; appreciation and celebration of art/music; insightful, reflective, nostalgic; creative sensibility reflected by poetic rhythm and vivid **imagery**.

Over to you: Make

Answer the following Leaving Certificate question using the tips and techniques below.

QUESTION B

'Early-in-life experience has been central to me.'

Imagine yourself fifty years from now. You have achieved great success and public recognition in your chosen career. Write the text of **an interview** (questions and answers) about the experiences and influences in your youth that contributed to your later success. (50)

Answer tips

Present your answer in an interview format (two or more questions and answers). Allow the content and style to range broadly (informative, **narrative**, discursive, humorous and so forth) but keep your questions and answers focused on the experiences and influences that contributed to later success.

Evidence of the following will be rewarded:

- Clear appreciation of the task
- Consistency of **register**
- Sense of audience/reader
- Quality of your questions and answers.

Techniques: Interview

- Include a brief introduction outlining who the interviewer is, who the interviewee is and the context or reasons for the interview.

- Write the interview in a question and answer format.

- Devise questions that <u>elicit</u> detailed responses.

- Offer detailed answers that include **anecdote** and descriptive writing. In this way the personality of the interviewee will be revealed.

- Remember that an interview is a written transcript of a spoken exchange. The **register** should, therefore, be relaxed and casual.

Test yourself

This text is adapted from a **blog** maintained by the English writer, actor, humorist and Norwich City Football Club director, Stephen Fry. In it he writes about his surprising love of football.

'An Open Letter to All Who Despise Sport and Especially Football' by Stephen Fry

My love of all kinds of sport surprises nobody more than myself. I do not think there has ever been a schoolboy with such overmastering contempt, fear, dread, loathing, and hatred for "games" – for sport, exercise, gymnastics and physical exertions of all or any kinds. Every day I would wake up with a sick jolt wondering just how I might get out of that day's compulsory rugby, cricket, hockey, swimming or whatever foul healthy horror was due to be posted on the notice-board that morning. The catalogue of multiple lies, evasions, self-imposed asthma attacks and other examples [of] what Edwardian school fiction characterised as "lead-swinging", <u>malingering</u> and "cutting". All the acts of a cad, a swine, a rotter, an outsider and a beast.

This hatred, as is so often the way with extremism, was to be replaced with an almost equal and opposite love. But before I came round to sport, largely through watching cricket, I had always, even through my most <u>indolent</u>, <u>fey</u>, camp, furious and <u>posturing</u> anti-athletic phases, avidly scanned the back pages of newspapers to follow the fortunes of Norwich City Football Club.

I don't know why this is. I came from a household that showed as much knowledge or interest in sport as hedgehogs show in embroidery. True, my mother had kept goal for England schoolgirls at hockey and my brother had shot for the school at Bisley, but beyond that the Fry household had as much interest or understanding of sport as a potato has of <u>Riemann's zeta function</u>. There was no contempt, just absolute indifference and incomprehension. But . . .

I have always had, to a frankly stupid degree, a deep sense of loyalty and connection. I came from East Anglia, therefore East Anglia was the best part of Britain. It was natural to me then that my heart would leap when it heard or saw the word "Norwich" on the national news. And the only time that could ever happen was when the football scores were read or printed.

Football is our national game. The beautiful game. And so on. There's so much wrong with it. The corporations and holding companies who own the clubs. Their obsession with European silverware. The stinkingly vast sums paid out by broadcasters. The vast gap between the oligarchic haves and the deprived have-nots.

If you have always found yourself immune to the national obsession with Association Football, I can quite understand it. But all I would say is that, for all that is wrong with it, there can be no keener pleasure than belonging, adhering, following and obsessing with one club: scrabbling for the latest news, checking with terror the tables to see how far they are from relegation and despair. The club can be Chelsea if you have reason for it to be. It can also be Gillingham or Port Vale, York City or Newcastle. If you already have a club that you support, then you don't need [to] read any further. But let's suppose that you don't support any club. Well, if you have a spare sense of loyalty going, an impulse to follow without a special connection, then let me suggest that you find a delightful underdog to cheer on . . .

Let me, in short, argue that you simply could not choose a more loveable and worthy club than Norwich City. They represent a whole region, one great medieval city lost in the rural vastness of Norfolk. Once among the two or three greatest towns of England, Norwich has almost comically lost itself in provincial isolation while the industrial cities of the North and Midlands, Manchester, Leeds, Liverpool, Birmingham, Stoke and Wolverhampton, and the powerful metropolitan districts, Arsenal, Tottenham, Chelsea, Queen's Park and Fulham have overtaken the game with their colossal financial and media reach.

Norwich is a pigmy compared to these enormous, illustrious and opulent institutions. That is what makes being a fan such a pleasure. We don't expect to win every match – when we do we jump up and down with joy and when we lose we smile ruefully as we expected nothing more.

There was no prouder moment for me than when I was asked to join Norwich's board of directors. I can bring neither football nor financial expertise to the table, but I can bring that element of loyalty, devotion and local passion that I hope and believe is a great part of what makes football the most popular game on earth.

Should you, I repeat, have a spare shred of unattached allegiance in you, then why not affix it to the club that has the oldest song in footballing history?

QUESTION A

(i) What, in your opinion, are the main reasons that 'makes being a fan such a pleasure' for Stephen Fry? Support your view with reference to the text. (15)

(ii) Stephen Fry's followers on Twitter exceeded six million in 2014. Based on your reading of the above text (content and style), what is it about Fry's personality that makes him so popular? (15)

(iii) 'The key features of the blog are an immediate and conversational tone, and a relaxed, informal register.' Discuss this statement with reference to the content and style of Stephen Fry's blog. (20)

QUESTION B

'. . . there can be no keener pleasure . . .'

You have been asked to contribute **a blog** to your school website, in which you describe what you enjoy most in films **or** in TV **or** in gaming. Write the text of your first post for this blog. (50)

Personal WRITING

Diary and letter

Introduction

A **diary** is a record, originally in handwritten format, with discrete entries arranged by date, reporting on what has happened over the course of a day or other period. A personal diary may include a person's experiences and/or thoughts or feelings, including comments on current events. Someone who keeps a diary is known as a diarist.

Generally, diaries are intended to remain private or to have a limited circulation amongst friends or relatives. Diaries are sometimes referred to as 'journals', but generally a diary has daily entries, whereas journal entries can be less frequent.

Although a diary may provide information for a **memoir**, **autobiography** or **biography**, it is not usually written with the intention of being published. Rather, it is usually intended for the author's personal use. However, many diaries and journals of notable figures have been published and form an important element of autobiographical literature.

Diary is also a popular form for fiction. Famous recent examples of works of fiction presented in diary mode include the *Adrian Mole* series by Sue Townsend and *Bridget Jones's Diary* by Helen Fielding. The diary format is also frequently used as a device within fiction. It is an excellent device for revealing a character's inner thoughts and feelings. A good example of this is Tom Riddle's diary in *Harry Potter and the Chamber of Secrets* by J. K. Rowling. Diary entries are also a feature of the **epistolary** novel, a novel written as a series of documents.

A **letter** is a written message containing information from one party to another. Historically, letters, in paper form, were the only reliable means of communication between two people in different locations. As communication technology has diversified, posted letters have become less important as a routine form of communication, and email, text messaging and Twitter have greatly reduced the practice of personal letter writing. However, letters remain appropriate for many purposes and they are still valued today.

Letters, whether formal or informal, private or public, offer a fascinating glimpse into the life and world of the letter-writer. The poet Emily Dickinson said that 'a letter always feels to me like immortality because it is the mind alone'. The very moment that the person wrote it and the thoughts and feelings of the writer at that particular time give the writing immediacy. A famous example of the use of letters in literature occurs in Mary Shelley's epistolary novel *Frankenstein*, published in 1818.

READ–ANALYSE–MAKE

A Woman in Berlin is the published **diary** of an anonymous woman who lived in the German city during the closing months of World War II, when the city was sacked by the Russian Army. In the diary she records and meditates on her harrowing experiences.

READ

from *A Woman in Berlin* (anonymous)

TUESDAY, 24 APRIL 1945, AROUND NOON

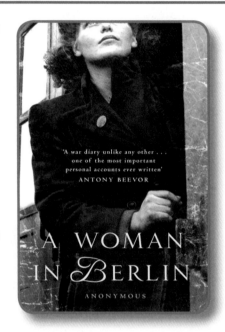

No news. We're completely cut off. Some gas but no water. Looking out of the window I see throngs of people outside the stores. They're still fighting over the rancid butter – they're still giving it away, but now it's down to a quarter of a pound per ration card. The schutzpolizei are just now getting things under control – I see four of them. And on top of that it's raining.

At the moment I'm sitting on the window seat in the widow's apartment. She just stormed in, all worked up. A shell hit outside Hefter's meat market, right in the middle of the queue. Three dead and ten wounded, but they're already queuing up again. The widow demonstrated how people were using their sleeves to wipe the blood off their meat coupons. 'Anyway, only three people died,' she said. 'What's that compared to an air raid?' No question about it: we're spoiled, all right.

Still, I'm astounded at how the sight of a few beef quarters and hog jowls is enough to get the frailest grandmother to hold her ground. The same people who used to run for shelter if three fighter planes were spotted somewhere over central Germany are now standing in the meat line as solid as walls. At most they'll plop a bucket on their head or perhaps a helmet. Queuing is a family business, with every member on shift for a couple of hours before being relieved. But the line for meat is too long for me; I'm not yet ready to give it a go. Besides, meat has to be eaten right away; it won't keep for more than a meal. I think they're all dreaming of eating their fill one last time, a final meal before the execution.

2 p.m. Just caught a glimpse of the sun. Without giving it a second thought, I strolled out to the balcony overlooking the courtyard and sat down in my wicker chair, basking in the sun – until a formation of bombers whizzed by overhead and one explosion merged into the next. I'd actually forgotten there was a war on. As it is, my head is oddly empty – just now I jerked up from my writing, something fell close by, and I heard the clink of shattering glass. Once again I'm having hunger pangs on a full stomach. I feel the need to gnaw on something. What's the baby who's still nursing supposed to live off now, the baby who can't get any milk? Yesterday the people who were queuing up were talking about children dying. One old lady suggested that a piece of bread chewed up and full of saliva might help the little ones when they can't get any milk.

An infant in the city is a sorry thing indeed, when its elaborately constructed supply of milk has been disrupted. Even if the mother manages to find something for herself and get halfway nourished, the source is bound to run dry soon enough, given what is approaching us so mercilessly. Fortunately the youngest child in our basement is already eighteen months old. Yesterday I saw someone slip the mother a couple of biscuits for the baby – in what was likely the only recent act of giving. Mostly people squirrel away whatever they have and nobody thinks about sharing anything with anybody.

Back in the basement, 9 p.m. Towards evening a woman we didn't know showed up and asked the widow and me to go with her to help in the field hospital.

Smoke and red skies on the horizon. The east is all ablaze. They say the Russians have already reached Braunauer Strasse – **ironic**, considering that it was in Braunau that Adolf first saw the light of day.

Written text

The entry for the **diary** is exact: it states the day, date and time. Information is recorded in brief, telegrammatic communications such as, 'Some gas but no water.' The use of the present tense adds to the immediacy of the scene being captured. As befits the private nature of the **genre**, the language is informal.

The second paragraph contains an account of an incident witnessed by a woman referred to as 'the widow', in whose apartment the author is staying. The widow's chilling **reportage** – 'only three people died. What's that compared to an air raid?' – provides a powerful insight into the reality of life during wartime.

As well as recording events, the author reflects on the human behaviour she witnesses: 'The same people who used to run for shelter . . . are now standing in the meat line as solid as walls.' Longer sentences characterise such reflective entries.

At 2 p.m. the author records her experience of sitting on a balcony, basking in the sunshine, when 'a formation of bombers whizzed by overhead'. Her own hunger leads her to think of others and a growing sense of desperation is evident in the open-ended question she asks about a nursing baby. The question leads to broader meditations and this paragraph concludes with the author offering a grim, but honest, assessment of human nature in times of crisis: 'nobody thinks about sharing anything with anybody'.

The final entry in the extract is recorded at 9 p.m. in the basement of the apartment block in which the author lives. In a text whose primary function is to record both the extraordinary events taking place and the author's reaction to them, **imagery** will be used sparingly and not merely as ornamentation. When employed, therefore, such images strike the reader as particularly vivid: for instance, 'Smoke and red skies on the horizon.' The entry ends on a foreboding note as the author reports rumours that 'the Russians have already reached Braunauer Strasse'.

Visual text

The **visual** text is a book cover for *A Woman in Berlin*, which features a photograph of a woman. The photo almost fills the **frame**, but is cut at the woman's eyes and lower body. Only her right side, including her right hand, is entirely within the frame. The woman is wearing a purple coat. Both the coat and the woman's hairstyle evoke the fashion of the 1940s. The woman is looking out from what appears to be the doorway of a tram, mauve in colour but mottled to indicate wear.

The title of the book is presented in a romantic-style white font; a quotation testifying to the historical importance of the text is also in a white font, albeit in a smaller size. The quotation has a central position on the book cover. The word 'ANONYMOUS' is smaller than the title and is printed in capital letters in a pink font. There is an unnerving **contrast** between the images associated with femininity on the front of the book – purple, pink, white romantic font – and the harrowing account of survival printed on the pages within.

The photo of the woman communicates powerful messages regarding the text of the book. The woman is young and attractive but, significantly, she is not positioned in a conventional way within the frame: parts of her body have been cut from it, which suggests disturbance or some deviation from the norm. The woman gazes upwards as though she is looking for something. For meaning? For salvation? For enemy aircraft? Her eyes are not entirely visible, perhaps indicating an inability to see the future. The woman is positioned in the doorway of a tram, symbolising possibly that she is on a journey, but certainly conferring on the image an ambiguous, transitional quality.

Finally, purple dominates this visual. It is the colour most associated with ambiguity since, like other colours made by combining two primary colours, it is seen as lacking certainty.

QUESTION B

Write **three diary entries** on your experiences (real or imaginary) of overcoming a challenge in your life. (50)

Sample answer

May 2nd

Dear Diary,

Today Ms Wilkins called me out of class and asked me to make the end-of-year speech on behalf of all the senior students in the school. I know it is an honour, but right now I feel under so much pressure. The exams are looming on the horizon and I'm worried that I won't live up to other people's expectations of me or, worse, that I'll let myself down. I know people see me as a confident, outgoing person, but inside I often feel insecure. It is as though I am two people, one extrovert and the other shy and sensitive. Maybe everyone feels like this. What am I going to do? I could go to Ms Wilkins and tell her I am too busy to give the speech but she'll think it strange that I said nothing today, just smiled and mumbled about it being an honour to be chosen. Why did I do that? I suppose that deep down I <u>am</u> honoured. O Diary, it would be great to make the end-of-year speech. I'm just not sure I can do it.

May 13th

Dear Diary,

I have decided to make the end-of-year speech. It is a huge personal challenge but I refuse to let negativity chip away at my burgeoning confidence. This is the new me! The day after my last diary entry I bought a copy of the book *Feel the Fear and Do It Anyway* by Susan Jeffers – and I read it cover to cover. The premise of the book is that we all feel fear, but we should take on challenges anyway. I also had a chat with Ms Wilkins and she suggested I join Toastmasters – so I did that too! They are an amazing group of people who get together to practise the art of public speaking. There are branches all over the country. O Diary, I am due to make the speech at 2 p.m. tomorrow in the school library. I have worked so hard, writing a good speech and practising over and over with the help of some of the inspirational people I've met in Toastmasters. Wish me luck!

May 14th, 9 p.m.

Dear Diary,

I did it! I made the speech to senior students and staff. The feedback was extremely positive and I have to admit, I am proud of myself. What a challenge to overcome! I'm still hearing bits and pieces of the speech in my ears, especially the quote from Nelson Mandela I used at the end: 'Education is the most powerful weapon you can use to change the world.' I could feel the atmosphere in the room when I finished speaking. It was electric! O Diary, I am so relieved. Hopefully I will carry this experience with me through life and learn from it. Now, I had better turn my attention back to that little thing called the Leaving Certificate.

Techniques: Diary

- As you are writing to yourself – a diary is a private document – your tone should be personal.
- Use casual language, including **colloquial** expression, which is part of the diary **register**.
- Employ descriptive language to report events and experiences clearly.
- Reflect on events and experiences in a thoughtful way.
- Although communication of feelings is part of the **genre** of diary writing, avoid an overly <u>confessional</u> approach.

Over to you: Read and analyse

As you read the following text from the 2011 Leaving Certificate exam paper, take note of the annotations in the margins and see if you can isolate the particular words and phrases that the annotations refer to. In this way you will improve your skills in both reading and analysing.

Personal WRITING

Text 1, 2011: Mystery

This text is taken from *An Irishwoman's Diary* by journalist, Lara Marlowe. She was *Irish Times* correspondent in Beirut and Paris, and is now based in Washington. Here she responds to an article critical of cats written by her friend and fellow journalist, Rosita Boland.

Strong personal statement serves as an introduction to the text

Use of short sentences adds to emphatic tone

I have venerated cats since early childhood. For more than two decades, Walter the Beirut Puss and now Spike the Irish Moggy, have enriched my life. There are people and possessions I could live without. But a cat is indispensable.

Concrete illustrations used to support point

Personal anecdote

Rosita Boland is a cherished friend and colleague but I could not allow her attack on the feline species, in a recent article, to go unanswered. Reading it here in Washington, I relived the disappointment – not to say sense of betrayal – that I felt years ago, when on a pilgrimage to Edith Wharton's home in Massachusetts, I discovered that the novelist regarded cats as "snakes in fur".

Context provided for writing article

Quotation employed to demonstrate point

Personal tone appeals to reader

I cannot say why reading a book is more pleasurable with a cat sitting in teapot mode at one's side or why I sleep better with Spike curled up at the foot of the bed, but it is so.

Interesting visual metaphor

Historical references broaden the scope of the article

I understand why the ancient Egyptians worshipped cats, and why medieval man burned them as witches. Something in cats surpasses their status as household pets: they are a mystery that eludes us. Victor Hugo wrote that "God invented the cat to give man the pleasure of petting a tiger". Every day Spike makes me laugh. I recall on the day my furniture arrived here from Paris, ten months ago, Spike purred triumphantly from the top of the sofa and rolled on his back on the living room carpet.

Literary allusion strengthens author's argument

Personal anecdote

Concrete detail adds authenticity to the text

Hyperbole adds to description

Now we enjoy watching the sparrows and doves that cavort in the magnolia trees surrounding our third-floor terrace in Georgetown. The pastime has its perils; when birds land on the balustrade, Spike's haunches quiver as he prepares to leap. I clap and scream to break his launch into the void.

Effective choice of verb

Alliteration used effectively to add to the gentle humour of the text

Further historical allusion

When I work, I recall the 8th-century Irish monk who hunted words while his cat, Pangur-Ban, hunted mice. The mouse in our apartment is attached to my computer, and Spike has an unfortunate habit of walking on the keyboard and obscuring the screen, just when I'm most desperately seeking the right phrase.

Lovely use of pun

Personal WRITING

Article moves seamlessly between informative and personal styles

Quotation effectively supports point

Creative use of verb

The visual text supports the written text in that it illustrates the close nature of the relationship between people and cats. However, the inquisitive and mischievous nature of cats, as described in the text, is not evident in this visual

Consider how much felines have given to art and literature. Foujita and Steinlen immortalised them on canvas. Ernest Hemingway kept 30 of them. Baudelaire's *The Cat*, as translated by Ulick O'Connor, explains how humans identify with felines: "He returns my gaze, careless what I discover and what do I find there, I find myself." Like me, Spike loves the feather duvet and fireside in winter. But like me, he's chronically restless. We zig-zag between boundless energy and exhaustion, and we share the journalist's most important characteristic, curiosity.

Image 1: *Julie Manet* de Pierre Auguste Renoir, Musée d'Orsay, Paris

Concrete illustrations add weight to argument

Analogy between cat and author is effectively communicated

The visual text is a portrait of a girl holding a cat. The use of colour in the painting is muted and impressionistic, adding to the serene quality of the image. Also, the girl's tranquil facial expression complements the relaxed pose of the cat as it luxuriates in the affection it receives

Personal anecdote

Use of italics and exclamation mark create an emphatic tone

Years ago, Zeinab, my Arabic teacher in Beirut, glanced at her Siamese cat Feyrouz who liked to sit in on my lessons. "Sometimes, you'd almost think they were thinking," Zeinab said. "*Of course* they are thinking!" I blurted out. I never doubted it for a moment.

Last week, I attended a Bloomsday celebration where actors read excerpts from *Ulysses*. I love the passage where Leopold Bloom prepares breakfast for Molly. "I never saw such a stupid pussens as the pussens," Bloom says. "Silly cat. You silly cat," I tell Spike several times daily.

Exchange of dialogue adds drama to the text

Personal anecdote

Further literary allusion

Joyce wrote of cats, "They understand what we say better than we understand them." If I was sad or discouraged, my previous cat, Walter, would sit quietly nearby. Perhaps it's his gender (Walter, despite her name, was female), but Spike is a good-time cat who has no patience for brooding. When I'm cheerful, his eyes light up. He

Vivid descriptions bring the text to life

performs celebratory leaps, makes a gurgling sound from the throat, and runs to the toy basket in the hope of a game of moussing.

Effective use of onomatopoeia

My favourite T-shirt bears a cat face drawn by Jean Cocteau, and the words "Friends of the cat". It's true; we cat-lovers recognise one another and exchange news of our moggies. Back in Paris, my

Variety of sentence lengths maintains a conversational tone

relations with a stern administrator at the Élysée Palace improved after I ran into her in the pet food section of a supermarket one Saturday morning.

Colloquial language emphasises affection for cats

I don't discriminate against non-cat lovers, though I must admit I had second thoughts about a recent visitor whom Spike hissed at. Tactful friends greet Spike with respect on arrival. Nothing so elaborate as, "Hail Majesté"; "Hello Spike" is sufficient.

Text ends on a humorous note

*The **visual** text illustrates some of the complexities dealt with in the written text. The body language of the cat captures many of the contrasting feline traits mentioned. The animal is relaxed (its back leg is draped over the balustrade) but also intensely alert (its slanted eyes are watchful)*

*This **visual** text depicts a cat on a balustrade. The painting is tonal. Various shades of green (particularly in the eyes and the leafy background) and brown are suggestive of the natural world, and create a sense of the 'mystery' of cats and their wildness, as described in the written text*

Image 2: *Summer: Cat on a Balustrade* by T. A. Steinlen, Museum of Fine Arts, Houston

Personal WRITING

Answer the following Leaving Certificate questions using the guidelines below.

QUESTION A

(i) From reading this article what impression do you form of the personality and lifestyle of Lara Marlowe? Support your view with reference to the text. (15)

(ii) Identify and comment on at least **two** stylistic features within the passage which you think add to the appeal of the text. (15)

(iii) Do you think that the two visual images effectively capture the different characteristics attributed to cats by Marlowe and others in the text? Explain your answer with detailed reference to both visual images. (20)

Answer guidelines

Part (i): begin by explicitly answering the question; for instance, *From reading this article I form a strong impression of the personality and lifestyle of Lara Marlowe*. Focus your answer on both the personality and lifestyle of Lara Marlowe, although not necessarily equally. Possible points include: sensitive and inquisitive nature; well read, with an artistic and philosophical outlook; whimsical, good sense of humour; outgoing, sociable, enjoys home comforts; urbane, cosmopolitan traveller.

Part (ii): begin by answering the question; for instance, *There are stylistic features within the passage that add to the appeal of the text*. Then explicitly identify at least two features of style that add to the appeal of the text. Include illustration and commentary on your chosen features. Possible points include: interesting references and quotations engage the reader; personal approach adds appeal; vivid, descriptive details and images heighten impact; lively and confident use of language entertains.

Part (iii): remember that questions on the **visual** text require an analysis of both content and style. Also, note that this question allows you to agree and/or disagree; answers that both agree and disagree with a question have more material to draw on. Begin by explicitly answering the question; for instance, *To a large extent, I think that the two visual images effectively capture the different characteristics attributed to cats by Marlowe and others in the written text*. You should make detailed references (though not necessarily equally) to both visual images in your response. Possible points include:

- Agree: comforting and protective; inscrutable – 'a mystery that eludes us'; sensual – 'a good-time cat'; restless, predatory, unpredictable – 'snakes in fur'
- Disagree: hunting skills, 'boundless energy'; silly antics – 'a stupid pussens'.

Over to you: Make

Answer the following Leaving Certificate question using the tips and techniques below.

QUESTION B

Places one has never visited often hold a certain mystery or fascination. Write a **feature article** for a travel magazine about a place you have never been to but would like to visit. In your article explain what you find fascinating about this place and why you would like to go there. (50)

Answer tips

Present your answer in the form of an article. There are a broad range of approaches to a feature article: personal, persuasive, informative, discursive, humorous and so on. Choose a style that suits you, but remember to adhere strongly to the terms of the question. Focus on what you find *fascinating* about the place you have chosen and *why* you would like to go there. The following will be rewarded:

- Clear appreciation of the task
- Consistency of **register**
- Enthusiastic approach
- Imaginative description
- Quality of your writing.

Techniques: Feature article

- Layout is an important feature of Question B tasks. Organise your answer in imitation of the general layout of a feature article: headline, subheading, **by-line**, reasonably short paragraphs.

- Choose your **register** to suit the particular style of the feature article you have decided to write – for example, personal, persuasive, informative, discursive, humorous – while maintaining a reasonably formal tone.
- Include descriptive **imagery** to bring your text to life for the reader.
- Remember, in all journalistic texts the essential quality is clarity of expression.

Test yourself

Philip Larkin was one of the foremost English poets of the twentieth century and his poetry often features on the Leaving Certificate syllabus. Larkin met Monica Jones when they were both twenty-four and she became his correspondent and lover until his death in 1985. In this letter, which Larkin sent to her while working as a librarian at Queen's University, Belfast, he writes about ordinary life and his concerns about his mother. Larkin and Jones are pictured above on holiday in the Isle of Sark, the smallest of the Channel Islands, in 1960.

Letter to Monica Jones from Philip Larkin

5 November 1950

Queen's Chamber, Belfast

Dearest M.,

Not on the whole a very satisfactory day. It's ten to five. I'm lying on my bed, having cleaned three pairs of shoes, still dressing-gowned from a stupefying bath earlier on. You can guess how warm the rooms are: I never have the fire on but I can lie in only my dressing gown and not feel cold. Very little has been done today. I spent this morning writing home, a job that becomes extremely difficult sometimes. In fact I expect it lies at the bottom of the day's unsatisfactoriness. My mother's patient attempts to find someone to live with so she need not bother either of us* make me very uncomfortable. When I lived with her I was consumed with desire to get away – it seemed a prime necessity, like breathing – but now I *am* away it seems very shabby & callous of both of us that she shd have to be bothering her head about advertisements and pretending to like people when really the ordeal of setting up house with a complete stranger will be as miserable to her as to me. I long to tell her to stop troubling & bring everything over here, but I know that it would be final self-destruction as far as I was concerned. It seems to me insulting to do anything else, as well as selfish and ungrateful, and it's no use not helping people when they need help on the grounds that someday it'll be possible to help them enjoyably . . . I do sincerely think that life with a really sympathetic personality wd do her more *good* than life with myself or my sister, but there are very few chances of finding such a person, & many more of finding cadgers, bores, mean spirits, & so on who will be difficult to displace once they are installed.

Well, that's enough about that particular aspect of my affairs: it will all boil up again at Christmas, as you can well imagine. I quite dread it: selfish again. O flames! Forgive me for bothering *you* about it.

I shall have to start dressing for supper in a couple of minutes – 5.45 on Sunday. I am wearing a suit today – gloomy conformity to local tradition. But most of the students here dress up on Sunday & look so neat that I get shamed: nearly every day of the week they wear semi-stiff white collars, the kind I wouldn't wear for a bob a day, & after all they are doctors-to-be & therefore I suppose quite well off. When anyone falls ill they are on him like a pack of vultures. Sometimes drunks are brought in to be resurrected medically before being sent home to their landladies.

Must dress. It's been a beautiful day but is now misty & coldish, & growing dark. [. . .]

* Larkin is referring here to himself and his sister

QUESTION A

 (i) Based on your reading of the above text, what impression do you form of the personality of Philip Larkin? Support your view with reference to the text. (15)

 (ii) From your reading of the text, how would you describe the relationship between Philip Larkin and Monica Jones? Support your answer with reference to both the content and style of the letter. (15)

 (iii) 'Philip Larkin is a writer whose work is characterised by detailed descriptions of ordinary life.' Based on your reading of the text, would you agree with this assessment? (20)

QUESTION B

'. . . it will all boil up again at Christmas . . .'

Write **three diary entries** in which you anticipate, with some reluctance, an inevitable event in your life. (50)

Personal essay

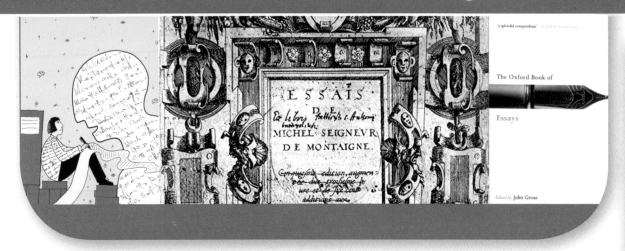

Introduction

The personal essay is one of the main composition types set on the Leaving Certificate exam paper. It has its roots in such writings as the letters of the Roman philosopher Seneca, but the first great practitioner of the **genre** was the sixteenth-century writer Michel de Montaigne, who coined the term *essai*, which literally means to try. This is what the personal essay is all about: trying to write honestly and accurately about life as you experience it.

Broadly speaking, there are two kinds of personal essay:

- The **narrative personal essay** is based on a detailed account of specific experiences. For instance, you might recall and describe your experiences, at various times, of listening to songs and being enthralled by the stories they tell. You are the main character. You are writing about ordinary things: people you know, places you have been to, experiences you have had. However, you must also offer the reader reflections on what insights, into yourself and into life, you have acquired from these experiences.

- The **discursive personal essay** takes as its starting point an abstract topic, and provides your reflections on this, while drawing on your personal experiences of life to illustrate your views. An example of a topic might be: the gap between the ideal world we can imagine and the real world we have to live in.

Both types of personal essay can feature on the Leaving Certificate HL exam paper.

Narrative and discursive personal essays share a common style, which William Hazlitt, one of the great essayists, termed a 'familiar style'. In an 1822 essay Hazlitt notes that 'to write in a truly familiar style is to write as any one would speak in a common conversation'. A familiar style, in other words, is a natural style, conversational and without pretence.

Techniques: Personal essay

- A personal essay is always written from a first person **point of view**.
- Essentially, a personal essay works best when it is true and honest. Draw on your experience of life and your knowledge of particular subjects.

- It is important that you are reflective. In this way you will reveal your personality.
- A personal essay should give the reader an insight into your inner self. It may contain thoughts, feelings, fears, hopes, likes, dislikes and so on.
- A personal essay can be private, like a **diary**, but it can also deal with broad issues, such as what it means to you to be young. If you select a discursive personal essay, make sure to transform the personal (experiences that are unique to you) into the universal (observations that are relevant to all of us).
- A personal essay may have a central story or a number of related stories, but the most important element is an insight into your thoughts and feelings and your response to the events described.
- However, you should shy away from a <u>confessional</u> approach that discloses intimate details of your emotional life; such an approach can descend very quickly into either sentimentality or sensationalism. Concentrate instead on more controlled description and philosophical musings.
- Remember to use **imagery** and detail to draw pictures in the reader's mind.
- Use a clear and logical structure for a discursive personal essay: introducing and then developing your theme; or a <u>chronological</u> sequence of events for a **narrative** personal essay: commenting on past events from your present standpoint.

READ-ANALYSE-MAKE: Personal Essay One (narrative)

Joan Didion was born in California in 1934. She has written five novels, but her most highly esteemed work is her **narrative** non-fiction, which she began writing in the 1960s in the form of essays. The following extract from the collection *Slouching Towards Bethlehem* demonstrates her acute powers of observation coupled with her ability to turn ordinary experience into art.

from 'Goodbye to All That' by Joan Didion

READ

It is easy to see the beginnings of things, and harder to see the ends. I can remember now, with a clarity that makes the nerves in the back of my neck constrict, when New York began for me, but I cannot lay my finger upon the moment it ended, can never cut through the <u>ambiguities</u> and second starts and broken resolves to the exact place on the page where the heroine is no longer as optimistic as she once was. When I first saw New York I was twenty, and it was summertime, and I got off a DC-7 at the old Idlewild temporary terminal in a new dress which had seemed very smart in Sacramento but seemed less smart already, even in the old Idlewild temporary terminal, and the warm air smelled of mildew and some instinct, programmed by all the movies I had ever seen and all the songs I had ever read about New York, informed me that it would never be quite the same again. In fact it never was.

Some time later there was a song in the jukeboxes on the Upper East Side that went "but where is the schoolgirl who used to be me," and if it was late enough at night I used to wonder that. I know now that almost everyone wonders something like that, sooner or later, and no matter what he or she is doing, but one of the mixed blessings of being twenty and twenty-one and even twenty-three is the conviction that nothing like this, all evidence to the contrary notwithstanding, has ever happened to anyone before.

Of course it might have been some other city, had circumstances been different and the time been different and had I been different, might have been Paris or Chicago or even San Francisco, but because I am talking about myself I am talking here about New York. That first night I opened my window on the bus into town and watched for the skyline, but all I could see were the wastes of Queens and big signs that said MIDTOWN TUNNEL THIS LANE and then a flood of summer rain (even that seemed remarkable and exotic, for I had come out of the West where there was no summer rain), and for the next three days I sat wrapped in blankets in a hotel room air conditioned to 35 degrees and tried to get over a cold and a high fever. It did not occur to me to call a doctor, because I knew none, and although it did occur to me to call the desk and ask that the air conditioner be turned off, I never called, because I did not know how much to tip whoever might come – was anyone ever so young? I am here to tell you that someone was. All I could do during those years was talk long-distance to the boy I already knew I would never marry in the spring. I would stay in New York, I told him, just six months, and I could see the Brooklyn Bridge from my window. As it turned out the bridge was the Triborough, and I stayed eight years.

In retrospect it seems to me that those days before I knew the names of all the bridges were happier than the ones that came later, but perhaps you will see that as we go along. Part of what I want to tell you is what it is like to be young in New York, how six months can become eight years with the deceptive ease of a film dissolve, for that is how those years appear to me now, in a long sequence of sentimental dissolves and old-fashioned trick shots—the Seagram Building fountains dissolve into snowflakes, I enter a revolving door at twenty and come out a good deal older, and on a different street. But most particularly I want to explain to you, and in the process perhaps to myself, why I no longer live in New York. It is often said that New York is a city for only the very rich and the very poor. It is less often said that New York is also, at least for those of us who came there from somewhere else, a city only for the very young.

This is an excellent example of the **narrative** personal essay. It begins with a very specific and very significant experience in the writer's life, a particular place, a particular moment: 'I can remember now . . . when New York began for me'. The opening sentence introduces this account and, incidentally, reminds us that the past is the territory covered by the narrative personal essay: 'It is easy to see the beginnings of things'.

Notice how the writing moves fluently back and forth between storytelling and personal reflection. On the one hand, we are told what actually happened and when, with Didion using very simple structural devices to tell her story in <u>chronological</u> sequence: 'When I first . . . Some time later . . . That first night . . . the next three days . . . I stayed eight years'. On the other, she is always reflecting on her own attitudes and feelings: 'I know now that almost everyone wonders something like that'. This combination illustrates the ideal approach to the narrative personal essay.

The other vital qualities of the narrative personal essay are clarity of expression and descriptive detail. Didion maintains clarity by writing in a familiar style, as though she is speaking truthfully to the reader, and by employing questions and a variety of sentence lengths. She brings the essay to life through descriptive detail, especially **sensory** images:

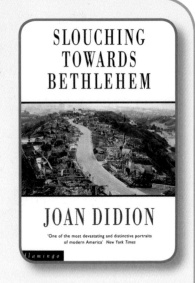

SLOUCHING TOWARDS BETHLEHEM

JOAN DIDION

'One of the most devastating and distinctive portraits of modern America' *New York Times*

- **Olfactory** image: 'warm air smelled of mildew'
- **Visual** image: 'all I could see were the wastes of Queens'
- **Tactile** image: 'I sat wrapped in blankets in a hotel room air conditioned to 35 degrees'.

MAKE

Write **a paragraph** describing a place that you consider to be atmospheric. Use the techniques below as a helping hand and, if you like, read the exemplar for inspiration!

Exemplar: A city at night

Viewed from a hotel bedroom, the city at night possesses a strange beauty. In the distance the jagged silhouette of skyscrapers is black and foreboding, with just a few office lights left on, like cat's eyes staring back. The sounds of the city in darkness are erratic and distant. I catch the bleat of an odd car horn and the faint hum of nightlife that sounds like the beat of a bass drum or a TV left on mute. A gentle breeze flutters by the window every so often, cooling my face and rippling through my hair. The smell of the river is in that breeze, algae and seaweed but also the detritus of the city, sewage and bilge. But from the tree-lined avenue below, the scent of leaves, opening their pores at the end of a long day, also wafts up to the balcony. This is the city at night, elegant and stained, a paradox.

Techniques: Writing about place

- Use the senses – **visual imagery**, **auditory imagery**, **olfactory imagery**, **tactile imagery** – to make your description feel three-dimensional.
- The writer Vladimir Nabokov coined the phrase 'caress the detail'. This means that you should provide accurate detail when describing setting; describe, for example, colours, textures and objects.

READ-ANALYSE-MAKE: Personal Essay Two (discursive)

Eric Arthur Blair, known by his pen name George Orwell, was an English novelist, journalist and essayist. Orwell wrote two of the most famous novels of the twentieth century, *Animal Farm* and *Nineteen Eighty-Four*. The term 'Orwellian' – descriptive of <u>totalitarian</u> practices – has entered the language together with several of his <u>neologisms</u>, including Cold War, Big Brother and thought police. The following extract is from an essay published in 1946.

from *Why I Write* by George Orwell

From a very early age, perhaps the age of five or six, I knew that when I grew up I should be a writer. Between the ages of about seventeen and twenty-four I tried to abandon this idea, but I did so with the consciousness that I was outraging my true nature and that sooner or later I should have to settle down and write books.

I was the middle child of three, but there was a gap of five years on either side, and I barely saw my father before I was eight. For this and other reasons I was somewhat lonely, and I soon developed disagreeable mannerisms which made me unpopular throughout my schooldays. I had the lonely child's habit of making up stories and holding conversations with imaginary persons, and I think from the very start my literary ambitions were mixed up with the feeling of being isolated and undervalued. I knew that I had a facility with words and a power of facing unpleasant facts, and I felt that this created a sort of private world in which I could get my own back for my failure in everyday life. Nevertheless the volume of serious—i.e. seriously intended—writing which I produced all through my childhood and boyhood would not amount to half a dozen pages. I wrote my first poem at the age of four or five, my mother taking it down to dictation. I cannot remember anything about it except that it was about a tiger and the tiger had 'chair-like teeth'—a good enough phrase, but I fancy the poem was a <u>plagiarism</u> of Blake's 'Tiger, Tiger'. At eleven, when the war of 1914–18 broke out, I wrote a patriotic poem which was printed in the local newspaper, as was another, two years later, on the death of Kitchener. From time to time, when I was a bit older, I wrote bad and usually unfinished 'nature poems' in the Georgian style. I also attempted a short story which was a ghastly failure. That was the total of the would-be serious work that I actually set down on paper during all those years.

However, throughout this time I did in a sense engage in literary activities. To begin with there was the made-to-order stuff which I produced quickly, easily and without much pleasure to myself. Apart from school work, I wrote *vers d'occasion*, semi-comic poems which I could turn out at what now seems to me astonishing speed—at fourteen I wrote a whole rhyming play, in imitation of Aristophanes, in about a week—and helped to edit school magazines, both printed and in manuscript. These magazines were the most pitiful <u>burlesque</u> stuff that you could imagine, and I took far less trouble with them than I now would with the cheapest journalism. But side by side with all this, for fifteen years or more, I was carrying out a literary exercise of a quite different kind: this was the making up of a continuous 'story' about myself, a sort of diary existing only in the mind. I believe this is a common habit of children and adolescents. As a very small child I used to imagine that I was, say, Robin Hood, and picture myself as the hero of thrilling adventures, but quite soon my 'story' ceased to be <u>narcissistic</u> in a crude way and became more and more a mere description of what I was doing and the things I saw. For minutes at a time this kind of thing would be running through my head: 'He pushed the door open and entered the room. A yellow beam of sunlight, filtering through the muslin curtains, slanted on to the table, where a match-box, half-open, lay beside the inkpot. With his right hand in his pocket he moved across to the window. Down in the street a tortoiseshell cat was chasing a dead leaf', etc. etc. This habit continued until I was about twenty-five, right through my non-literary years. Although I had to search, and did search, for the right words, I seemed to be making this descriptive effort almost against my will, under a kind of compulsion from outside. The 'story' must, I suppose, have reflected the styles of the various writers I admired at different ages, but so far as I remember it always had the same <u>meticulous</u> descriptive quality.

When I was about sixteen I suddenly discovered the joy of mere words, i.e. the sounds and associations of words. The lines from *Paradise Lost*,

> So hee with difficulty and labour hard
> Moved on: with difficulty and labour hee.

which do not now seem to me so very wonderful, sent shivers down my backbone; and the spelling 'hee' for 'he' was an added pleasure. As for the need to describe things, I knew all about it already. So it is clear what kind of books I wanted to write, in so far as I could be said to want to write books at that time. I wanted to write enormous naturalistic novels with unhappy endings, full of detailed descriptions and arresting similes, and also full of purple passages in which words were used partly for the sake of their own sound. And in fact my first completed novel, *Burmese Days*, which I wrote when I was thirty but projected much earlier, is rather that kind of book.

ANALYSE

This is an excellent example of the discursive personal essay. It begins with a sentence that introduces the theme of the essay: being a writer. Notice that Orwell is not interested in the <u>chronological</u> sequence of particular events, but in understanding both his own personality and what 'being a writer' actually means for him. He focuses, therefore, on what is common to large periods of time, rather than on what is unique to a specific moment. He introduces and then develops his theme with a consistent focus: 'From a very early age . . . I knew . . . I should be a writer', 'I had the lonely child's habit of making up stories', 'this was the making up of a continuous "story" about myself'.

Although specific **anecdotes** are not used at the beginning, in case they distract from the introduction of the theme, Orwell later describes particular experiences in order to illustrate his reflections: 'At eleven, when the war of 1914–18 broke out, I wrote a patriotic poem', 'For minutes at a time this kind of thing would be running through my head'. This combination illustrates the ideal approach to the discursive personal essay.

The other vital qualities of the discursive personal essay are clarity of expression and an honest tone. Orwell maintains clarity by writing in a familiar style, as though he is speaking to the reader, and by employing references and quotes to illustrate his reflections. He makes the essay more appealing and interesting by maintaining an honest tone throughout: 'I soon developed disagreeable mannerisms which made me unpopular throughout my schooldays'.

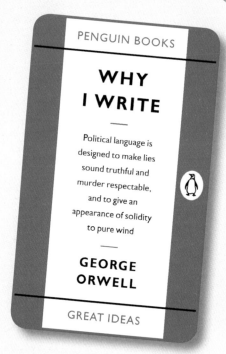

PENGUIN BOOKS

WHY
I WRITE

—

Political language is designed to make lies sound truthful and murder respectable, and to give an appearance of solidity to pure wind

—

GEORGE
ORWELL

GREAT IDEAS

Personal WRITING

Write **a paragraph** describing a person whom you know. Use the techniques below as a helping hand and, if you like, read the exemplar for inspiration!

Exemplar: My grandmother

My grandmother is a busy woman. One of her favourite sayings is 'the devil makes work for idle hands'. From morning until evening she bustles through the house and garden, making cakes, pulling weeds. I love sitting at the kitchen table, drinking a cup of tea, watching her in full flight. She is a small woman, spry as a bird, and always neatly turned out in pastel-coloured cardigans. When my grandmother is concentrating, her face takes on a comical expression, although no one would dream of telling her so. Her eyebrows rise to meet her hairline and her glasses slip to the very end of her nose. My grandmother is a great person to talk to. She is practically minded and nothing shocks her, and when she has something really important to say she always places her hand on her heart.

MAKE

Techniques: Writing about people

- Description: choose a detail that is unique to the person.
- Facial expression: capture personality by describing a particular facial expression.
- Body language: show how people reveal their true selves through movement.
- Action: say what your character is doing (for example, walking, watching television, humming a tune).
- **Dialogue**: give an insight into characters by capturing how they speak as well as what they say.

Personal WRITING

Exam tips for personal essays

Although the instructions to Leaving Certificate correctors repeatedly stress that candidates may choose to write their essays wholly or partly as personal **narratives**, it is clear from the various reports of Chief Examiners that the more reflection you provide, the greater the chance you have of writing a successful personal essay. Whether you choose to write a narrative personal essay (a true story about your life) or a discursive personal essay (an honest account of your knowledge, opinions and feelings in relation to a particular subject), the essential requirement is that you include reflection.

Instructions to correctors in the marking schemes of Leaving Certificate 2008–2012 personal essay compositions

2008

Question 4: 'I have a beautiful view . . .' Write a personal essay in which you describe a place that you consider beautiful.

Instruction to correctors: Candidates may choose to write their essays wholly or partly as personal narratives, but they should also include a descriptive and/or reflective element. Allow for a liberal interpretation of 'a place'.

Chief Examiner's remarks: This was quite a popular option, with the quality of responses ranging from insightful reflection to less engaging narrative. The most successful attempts avoided sentimentality and expressed genuine affection for particular places. Examiners noted some confusion in relation to the personal essay **genre**.

Question 6: 'I was happy . . .' Write an article for a school magazine in which you explore aspects of life that make you happy.

Instruction to correctors: Expect candidates to use a **register** suitable for a school magazine in shaping a personal response to one or more aspects of life 'that make you happy'. They may choose to adopt a wide variety of approaches – reflective, informative, narrative, humorous, **ironic**, etc.

Chief Examiner's remarks: This was not a popular choice. Personal narrative dominated and examiners reported marking a number of heartfelt pieces. The better essays conveyed a strong sense of personality and engaged well with the reader – often through the use of self-deprecating humour.

2009

Question 1: '. . . a living classroom . . .' Write an article (serious and/or light-hearted) for a school magazine about your experience of education over the last number of years.

Instruction to correctors: Reward a clearly established register and sense of audience appropriate to a school magazine. Allow for a liberal interpretation of 'education'.

Question 6: '. . . the dreamtime of my own imaginings.' Write a personal essay on the topic of daydreams.

Instruction to correctors: Expect a wide range of responses in terms of content and register. Candidates may choose to adopt various approaches – discursive, descriptive, humorous, personal narrative, etc., but they should include a reflective element in their treatment of the topic of daydreams.

2010

Question 1: '. . . it was terrific theatre . . .' Write a personal essay about your experience (as performer and/or audience member) of the dramatic arts: plays, musicals, concerts, comedy, etc.

Instruction to correctors: Expect a wide range of responses in terms of content and register in writing about one or more performances/experiences. Candidates may choose to adopt various approaches (personal narrative, discursive, descriptive, humorous, etc.) but they should include a reflective element.

Question 4: '. . . a certain freedom . . .' Write a personal essay about your understanding of freedom and why you think it is important.

Instruction to correctors: Expect a wide range of responses in terms of content and register. Candidates may choose to adopt various approaches (personal narrative, discursive, descriptive, humorous, etc.) but they should include a reflective element in their responses.

2011

Question 1: 'There are people and possessions I could live without. But a cat is indispensable.' You have been asked to speak to your class about what you think is indispensable in your life. Write the text of the talk you would give.

Instruction to correctors: Reward clear evidence of appropriate register and awareness of audience. Allow a broad interpretation of 'indispensable in your life'. Expect a variety of approaches – personal, persuasive, discursive, **anecdotal**, ironic, etc.

Question 5: 'My favourite T-shirt . . .' Write a personal essay about your clothes, what they mean to you and what they say about you.

Instruction to correctors: Candidates may choose to adopt various approaches – discursive, descriptive, humorous, personal narrative, etc. However, they should include a reflective element, and refer to both parts of the question, though not necessarily equally.

2012

Question 1: 'Yet the outside world had its continuing marvels . . .' Write a personal essay on what you consider to be the marvels of today's world.

Instruction to correctors: Allow for a broad interpretation of 'marvels of today's world'. Candidates may choose to adopt various approaches (personal, persuasive, discursive, anecdotal, ironic, etc.), but they should include a reflective element.

READ-ANALYSE-MAKE

Read the personal essay below, written by a sixth-year student in response to the task:

'Goodbye to All That . . .'

Write a personal essay on the topic of leaving.

Personal WRITING

READ

Student exemplar: Leaving

The act of leaving, and the emotions it brings with it, is one of the most universal experiences in our society. Felt on countless levels – physically, spiritually, permanently or temporarily – we have all left things, people and places and we have all experienced things, people and places leaving us. In almost every case there is no black-and-white emotion to sum up our feelings – leaving a loved one or losing a friend does not simply result in sadness, for instance, but often regret and anger or sometimes relief. Fully explaining the concept of 'leaving' would not be possible within the boundaries of a book, let alone an essay, but I will attempt to paint a picture of what it means to me.

Before she moved out, I lived with my sister for sixteen years and eleven months. I will not deny missing her presence, as both a sister and a close friend, but with her weekly visits, the change was not enormous. It is only when I study in her old bedroom that her absence is truly felt. The room, with a bed, an empty wardrobe, large bookshelf and a bare desk, is like a skeleton, lacking soul, lacking purpose. Sounds from outside and the TV downstairs rise through the floor and bounce off the bare walls, once covered in photographs, creating a quiet, ghostly echo. A thin layer of dust has formed on the bookshelf. The books, which were once removed and replaced regularly, sit still, wondering where my sister is and when she will return. The bed is still made. In an eerie way I am not comfortable sitting in the room. It is like a living creature that has grinded to a halt without its owner. The dead stillness is a constant reminder that something has left and cannot be replaced.

One can easily leave a place physically but does one's spirit ever truly depart somewhere forever? I have now finished thirteen years of my education in two schools, in both of which my picture hangs. Along with thousands of other boys, I entered my school and left and one day I may forget what it was like there, but I will always have fragments to hang on to. Possibly certain teachers or the annoyingly squeaky floor – a part of the school will always be in my mind. On the other hand, the school will always have a part of me, whether it is a simple scribble on the desk or a trivial award listed in my name. I have left, but it remains a place of memories, a breeding ground for nostalgia. Perhaps in many years when I have left this life my spirit will wander the cold corridors, the busy yard and the many classrooms in which I spent the days of my youth.

These questions remind me of the incredible uncertainty that comes with leaving somewhere. From the insignificant ones such as 'Will it rain if I go out without a coat?' To the more important 'Should I leave a job I'm wasting my life at?' And perhaps the greatest question of all time 'What happens when I leave this life?' These questions frighten us and because of this we yearn for company – friends to go abroad with, family to spend holidays with and partners for the long-term, life-changing decisions. We leave things every day but we are afraid to do it alone. Now as I leave my childhood behind and enter adulthood, where I have to worry about bank accounts, driving tests and student fees, I still have the same best friend I had in junior infants. With such huge changes on the horizon, having something familiar in my life makes it easier to face the uncertainties of leaving.

There are some things I could never leave. My childhood dreams are a good example, and the older I get the more I realise that I will never be an idolised footballer or a famous musician. Maybe this is a flaw, a barrier to realistic developments in my life, but I fear that when I'm thirty years old I will turn around and see a pile of ash at my feet formed from the charred remains of the dreams I had as a child. I could never leave behind the small golden compass gathering dust on my shelf, given to me by my father after my Junior Certificate – a reminder of the pride I instilled in him at the time. I can't let go of the small digital clock that tells me the time in every time zone and whose single battery I've replaced not once in eight years. The clock brings a sense of certainty with it, always waking me up, telling me the time on those nights when the heat suffocates and your mind works in overdrive preventing you from getting any sleep. The old photographs, postcards, collectable stickers from the 2002 World Cup, which occupied most of my summer all those years ago, are the small, unimportant objects that are just too difficult for me to let go.

Leaving comes in many forms and we leave things every day. But, whether we leave things for better or for worse, it's important that we keep some memories, maybe to guide us in the future or maybe to prevent us from repeating mistakes we made in our past. One day everyone alive right at this instant will be gone, but our generation's mark will remain on this world until the end of time. Every room, every street, every life you've stumbled into and left will always have a mark on it, however tiny. Even when we leave this world and everything in it forever, we are never completely gone.

ANALYSE

This is an excellent example of a discursive personal essay. It follows the recommended approach of introducing the theme: 'The act of leaving, and the emotions it brings with it, is one of the most universal experiences in our society'; and then developing it with a consistent focus: 'One can easily leave a place physically but does one's spirit ever truly depart somewhere forever?', 'These questions remind me of the incredible uncertainty that comes with leaving somewhere.'

Although **anecdotes** are not used at the beginning, in case they distract from the introduction of the theme, specific incidents are described throughout to illustrate the writer's reflections: 'Along with thousands of other boys, I entered my school', 'Now as I leave my childhood behind and enter adulthood'.

The writer maintains clarity of expression by writing in a familiar style, as though he is speaking truthfully to the reader.

Finally, he brings the essay to life through descriptive detail:

- **Simile**: the room 'is like a skeleton'
- **Auditory imagery**: 'creating a quiet, ghostly echo'
- Use of questions: 'What happens when I leave this life?'
- Use of lists: 'old photographs, postcards, collectable stickers'.

Personal WRITING

MAKE

Write **a narrative personal essay** about a significant event in your life using the following structure as a helping hand.

> Opening (1 paragraph): begin your essay by describing a specific and significant experience.

> Development (3–7 paragraphs): describe in detail what actually happened, while consistently reflecting on your own attitudes and insights. Remember to maintain a familiar style and an honest tone and to bring the essay to life with descriptive detail.

> Conclusion (1 paragraph): end your essay by bringing the narrative to a close and providing your final thoughts on why the experience is significant in your life.

Over to you: Make

Write a personal essay on any of the following:

1 '. . . for that is how those years appear to me now . . .' ('Goodbye to All That')

   Write a personal essay on the role of memory in our lives.

2 'As a very small child I used to imagine that I was, say, Robin Hood . . .' (*Why I Write*)

   Write a personal essay on 'Everyday Heroes'.

3 'My childhood dreams are a good example . . .' ('Leaving')

   Write a personal essay on the importance of dreams in our lives.

4 '. . . I soon developed disagreeable mannerisms . . .' (*Why I Write*)

   Write a personal essay on the things about yourself that you would most like to change.

5 'When I first saw New York I was twenty.' ('Goodbye to All That')

   Write a personal essay using the title 'Travel Broadens the Mind'.

> **Remember**
>
> Leaving Certificate compositions should be between 750 and 1,000 words. You have ten minutes to plan your composition and one hour to write it. The most important criteria for achieving a good grade are that you write consistently on the title you have chosen and that you use a **register** that suits the **genre** of the title. After that, marks are awarded for good structure and paragraphing, clear and fluent expression and correct grammar and spelling.

Discursive

WR!T!NG

 Speech and talk

 Review and debate

 Article and report

 Discursive essay

Speech and talk

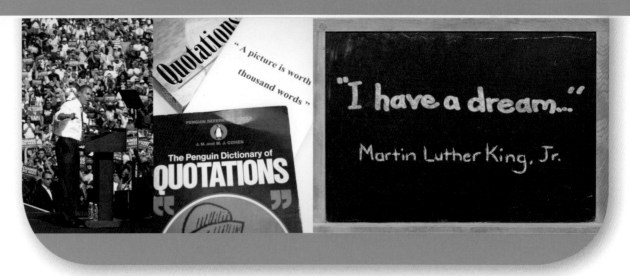

Introduction

In this unit you will be introduced to **speeches** and **talks**. Both speeches and talks have their origins in the art and practice of formal speaking in public, which is known as oratory and was taught in schools in ancient Rome and Greece. Rhetoric is similar to oratory but refers to the art and practice of both speaking and writing, and includes a persuasive element. Speeches are made on many occasions in life: from wedding speeches, to political speeches, to speeches made at special ceremonies.

While speeches may be delivered in a variety of tones – funny, serious, light-hearted, inspirational – the **register** of the **genre** is always formal. Talks, on the other hand, are often delivered in a casual setting, such as a classroom or library, and generally have a more relaxed, informal register. For example, a school graduation speech is formal, whereas a talk given to a sports team prior to a match is informal.

Speeches and talks have a number of characteristics in common:

- The audience must be addressed at the outset.
- The theme should be introduced early and kept in focus throughout.
- Rhetorical devices must be employed. Rhetorical devices are features of style that help to express and support the speaker's **point of view**. These rhetorical devices will be explored and illustrated throughout the unit.

READ-ANALYSE-MAKE

In May 2011 Queen Elizabeth II made a state visit to the Republic of Ireland at the invitation of then President of Ireland, Mary McAleese. It was the first state visit of a British monarch since 1911. The following is the text of Queen Elizabeth's **speech** delivered at the Irish state dinner.

Speech at Dublin Castle by Queen Elizabeth II

A Uachtaráin agus a chairde (President and friends).

Prince Philip and I are delighted to be here, and to experience at first hand Ireland's world-famous hospitality.

Together we have much to celebrate: the ties between our people, the shared values, and the economic, business and cultural links that make us so much more than just neighbours, that make us firm friends and equal partners.

Madam President, speaking here in Dublin Castle it is impossible to ignore the weight of history, as it was yesterday when you and I laid wreaths at the Garden of Remembrance.

Indeed, so much of this visit reminds us of the complexity of our history, its many layers and traditions, but also the importance of forbearance and conciliation. Of being able to bow to the past, but not be bound by it.

Of course, the relationship has not always been straightforward; nor has the record over the centuries been entirely benign. It is a sad and regrettable reality that through history our islands have experienced more than their fair share of heartache, turbulence and loss.

These events have touched us all, many of us personally, and are a painful legacy. We can never forget those who have died or been injured, and their families. To all those who have suffered as a consequence of our troubled past I extend my sincere thoughts and deep sympathy. With the benefit of historical hindsight we can all see things which we would wish had been done differently or not at all. But it is also true that no one who looked to the future over the past centuries could have imagined the strength of the bonds that are now in place between the governments and the people of our two nations, the spirit of partnership that we now enjoy, and the lasting rapport between us. No one here this evening could doubt that heartfelt desire of our two nations.

What were once only hopes for the future have now come to pass; it is almost exactly thirteen years since the overwhelming majority of people in Ireland and Northern Ireland voted in favour of the agreement signed on Good Friday 1998, paving the way for Northern Ireland to become the exciting and inspirational place that it is today. I applaud the work of all those involved in the peace process,

Discursive WRITING

and of all those who support and nurture peace, including members of the police, the Gardaí, and the other emergency services, and those who work in the communities, the churches and charitable bodies like Co-operation Ireland. Taken together, their work not only serves as a basis for reconciliation between our people and communities, but it gives hope to other peacemakers across the world that through sustained effort, peace can and will prevail.

For the world moves on quickly. The challenges of the past have been replaced by new economic challenges which will demand the same imagination and courage. The lessons from the peace process are clear; whatever life throws at us, our individual responses will be all the stronger for working together and sharing the load.

There are other stories written daily across these islands which do not find their voice in solemn pages of history books, or newspaper headlines, but which are at the heart of our shared narrative. Many British families have members who live in this country, as many Irish families have close relatives in the United Kingdom.

These families share the two islands; they have visited each other and have come home to each other over the years. They are the ordinary people who yearned for the peace and understanding we now have between our two nations and between the communities within those two nations; a living testament to how much in common we have.

These ties of family, friendship and affection are our most precious resource. They are the lifeblood of the partnership across these islands, a golden thread that runs through all our joint successes so far, and all we will go on to achieve. They are a reminder that we have much to do together to build a future for all our grandchildren: the kind of future our grandparents could only dream of.

So we celebrate together the widespread spirit of goodwill and deep mutual understanding that has served to make the relationship more harmonious, close as good neighbours should always be.

ANALYSE

The opening address of a **speech** is important in setting the desired tone. Queen Elizabeth's use of the Irish language in her opening address did just that, creating a warm atmosphere between speaker and audience.

The theme of the speech – the relationship between Ireland and England, in the past, in the present and in the future – is introduced at the outset and the focus on this theme is maintained throughout the speech.

The speech employs many rhetorical devices that ensure its successful delivery and impact. The following rhetorical devices are particularly well employed in the speech:

- Varied sentence length helps to maintain a lively rhythm: 'For the world moves on quickly. The challenges of the past have been replaced by new economic challenges which will demand the same imagination and courage.'
- Repetition enforces the point being made; for example, the word 'history' is used three times in the first two paragraphs of the speech.

- Forceful language creates a tone of sincerity: 'our islands have experienced more than their fair share of heartache, turbulence and loss'.

- **Triadic structures** inject energy (by delivering points in sets of three): 'strength, vision and determination'.

- **Imagery** conjures **visual** pictures for the audience; for example, a **metaphor** is used to create the image of something precious that delicately, but strongly, links the two communities: 'a golden thread that runs through all our joint successes so far'.

- **Emotive** language is used to evoke a shared emotion: 'It is a sad and regrettable reality . . .'.

- **Concrete illustrations** support points made in the speech: 'I applaud the work of all those involved in the peace process . . . members of the police, the Gardaí, and the other emergency services . . .'.

Remember that it is never sufficient merely to identify a rhetorical device. You must always demonstrate *why* it is effective in expressing or supporting the speaker's point.

MAKE

Discursive WRITING

QUESTION B

You have been asked to give **a talk to your class** entitled 'I like the dreams of the future better than the history of the past', which is a quotation from Thomas Jefferson, the principal author of the American Declaration of Independence. Write the text of the talk you would deliver. (50)

Sample answer

Fellow classmates,

Thank you for coming along to the library today.

Now, I hope you're sitting comfortably because I'm going to talk to you about something Thomas Jefferson once said: 'I like the dreams of the future better than the history of the past'. Thomas Jefferson was the principal author of the Declaration of Independence and the third President of the United States – in other words, a pretty important guy.

Don't look so bored at the back. This is interesting stuff! And anyway, the alternative to listening to me is listening to Ms Murray (only joking Ms).

We all have dreams – dreams of our future lives, of winning *The X Factor* or playing for Manchester United . . . or of just getting out of the library. The thing is – whatever our dreams may be – they are precious. They sustain us when life gets tough, and help us get through double maths on Monday mornings. We cannot live without dreams. As the song says, 'Dream until your dreams come true'.

But, fellow classmates, we stand and we fall together. Our dreams of our future lives are not separate, isolated dreams. They are interconnected. We all live on the same planet (well, most of us), and we all share the future of that planet. What would we like to see if we looked into the future in a crystal ball: war? famine? inequality? No. That is the past. That is history. That is not the future we dream of.

Fellow classmates, we may think that our world, in twenty-first-century Ireland, is not a good one. We worry about the future, about economic recession and our employment prospects, and about which poets will come up on the Leaving Certificate English exam paper. But these worries are nothing compared with the history of the past. We live in peace, prosperity and freedom and, as Martin Luther King said in his famous speech, 'in spite of the difficulties and frustrations of the moment, I still have a dream'.

Fellow classmates, the history of the past – war, famine and inequality – is a dark one, and that is why I, for one, prefer the bright dreams of the future.

Thank you.

Now back to class!

Techniques: Talk

- A talk is much less formal than a **speech** and therefore a relaxed, casual **register** is appropriate.
- Address your audience and keep in mind at all times that they are in front of you.
- Introduce your theme at the outset of the talk.
- Maintain a light tone throughout your talk; use humour, **imagery** and **anecdote** to keep your talk lively and interesting.
- Employ rhetorical devices, such as questions, **triadic structures** and forceful language, to engage your audience.
- Try to finish your talk with a brief summary of your points and then thank your audience for listening to you.

Over to you: Read and analyse

As you read the following text from the 2012 Leaving Certificate exam paper, take note of the annotations in the margins and see if you can isolate the particular words and phrases that the annotations refer to. In this way you will improve your skills in both reading and analysing.

Text 2, 2012: Shared memories

This text consists of an edited extract from a **speech** delivered by former President Mary Robinson to an international conference on hunger. In it she considers the commemoration of the Irish famine of 1845 and explores how society's memory of the past, our collective social memory, shapes our response to contemporary issues.

Discursive WRITING

The Irish famine is an event which more than any other shaped us as a people. It defined our will to survive. It defined our sense of human vulnerability. It remains one of the strongest, most poignant links of memory and feeling that connects us to our diaspora.

Repetition used to emphasise concepts

Introduction of theme in opening sentence

Historians recognise that it is important, indeed imperative, that we the survivors, and future generations, should know about those who had no one to speak for them at the time of their greatest need and suffering. The story of the silent people should be heard. But the story is not confined just to Ireland. I think particularly of Charles Fanning's fine book, *The Exiles of Erin*, which painstakingly lays before its readers the stories of those who escaped from famine and came to the United States and began to make a new present, which has now become a shared past.

Exhortation: the use of language to incite and encourage

Reference used to support point

At the conclusion of another book which I have read with enormous interest – *The End of Hidden Ireland*, by Robert Scally – there is a striking and moving sentence. Describing the emigrants who set out on the desolate journey from Ireland to America, he writes, "Peering from the stern rather than the bow of the emigrant ship, that backward glance at the incongruous palms and gaily painted houses along the shore near Skibbereen was not only their last sight of Ireland but the first sight of themselves." It is the backward glance leading to self-knowledge which in this sentence is so striking.

Forceful language strengthens point

Use of quotation to illustrate point

Image 1: Detail from Famine Memorial, Dublin

The woman's facial expression is one of horror; her eyes gaze upwards with a haunting, searching stare; her mouth is slack; her face is thin and drawn

The background of the image is that of a blurred cityscape

The image is of a stone sculpture. It shows the face and torso of a woman. Her hands are stretched, one over the other, holding a bundle. It is not clear what the bundle contains, but the protective way she holds it and the horror of her expression suggest that she is clutching her infant child

We need to reflect carefully on the purpose of commemorating an event such as the famine. The terrible realities of our past hunger present themselves to us as nightmare images. The bailiff, the famine wall. The eviction. The workhouse. And yet how willing are we to negotiate those past images into the facts of present-day hunger? How ready are we to realise that what happened to us may have shaped our national identity, but it is not an experience confined to us as a people? How ready are we to see that the bailiff and the workhouse and the coffin ship have equally terrible equivalents in other countries for other peoples at this very moment?

Exhortation

Forceful language emphasises point

Concrete illustrations to support point

Rhetorical questions add energy and passion

Discursive WRITING

Discursive WRITING

*Both women are captured within the **frame** of the photograph, which suggests solidarity between them; the image of joined hands in the centre is a powerful **symbol** of unity*

The women make eye contact with each other, not the camera, creating the impression of a candid photo rather than a staged image

Image 2: Mary Robinson with Nadhifa Ibrahim Mohamed, a health-worker in Somalia

Interesting use of colour: warm tones reflect the warm interaction between the women

Mary Robinson's headscarf, accommodating to the culture she is in, is another indicator of the respectful, harmonious relationship depicted in the image

For every piece of economic knowledge our children gain about the crops exported from Ireland during the famine years, let them come to understand the harsh realities of today's markets which reinforce the poverty and helplessness of those who already experience hunger.

Link explicitly made between Ireland's past and the present realities of poverty in the world

Allusion used to support point

Let them learn, too, from the influence the famine has had on contemporary Irish poets. When Eavan Boland [in her poem, *The Famine Road*] reflects sadly on the limitation of the science of cartography because the famine road does not show up on the map, or Seamus Heaney writes: "and where potato diggers are/ you still smell the running sore" they are drawing inspiration from that dark moment of our past. They remind us that famine in our contemporary world also silences the culture of peoples who are portrayed to us all too often as mere statistics. That portrayal makes it easier for us to distance ourselves, to switch off.

Forceful language

*Heading employs forceful, **emotive** language to communicate its point*

Stark representation of the statistics supplied in the text

Rectangular blocks, in varying shades of red, suggest alarm and crisis

FACT: THE CRISIS IN THE HORN OF AFRICA IS UNLIKE ANY OTHER – DISPLACING, STARVING, KILLING OVER 13 MILLION PEOPLE

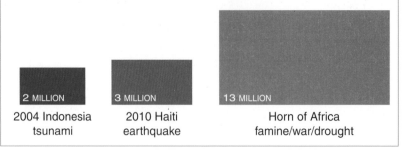

| 2 MILLION | 3 MILLION | 13 MILLION |
| 2004 Indonesia tsunami | 2010 Haiti earthquake | Horn of Africa famine/war/drought |

Image 3

*The **visual** informs us of the human cost of three natural disasters: the tsunami in Indonesia, the earthquake in Haiti, and famine, war and drought in the Horn of Africa*

If we are to account for the sheer horror of the disparity between twelve million children who died in the developing world in one year and the few hundred thousand it could have been if the world's

62

Repetition of word for emphasis

resources were better distributed, then we will need to send young people into the world who have been prepared to close the gap between the idea of hunger and the fact of it. We need to help young people to face the future with the understanding that famine is not something which can be understood only through history. It must be understood with every fibre of our moral being.

Answer the following Leaving Certificate questions using the guidelines below.

QUESTION A

(i) In the above extract, Mary Robinson explains why she thinks it is important to commemorate the Irish famine of 1845. Which **three** points from the text do you think most effectively support her viewpoint? In each case, briefly explain your choice. (15)

(ii) Identify and comment on **three** elements of effective speech-writing in Mary Robinson's address to the conference on hunger. In your answer you should refer only to the written text. (15)

(iii) Consider the three visual images that accompany this text. Which **two** of the images would you have chosen to project as a backdrop to Mary Robinson as she delivered the above speech? Explain your choice, discussing the impact you think these images would make on the audience. (In your answer, you should refer both to your chosen images and to the written text.) (20)

Answer guidelines

Part (i): begin by explicitly answering the question; for instance, *In her speech, Mary Robinson explains why she thinks it is important to commemorate the Irish famine of 1845. I have selected three points from the text which I think most effectively support her viewpoint. First . . .* Possible points include: informs our sense of national identity; provides a meaningful link to the diaspora; promotes awareness of contemporary issues; highlights how history can influence the present; encourages reflection, empathy and understanding.

Part (ii): begin by answering the question; for instance, *There are many elements of effective speech-writing in Mary Robinson's address to the conference on hunger . . .* Include illustration and commentary on three elements of speech-writing in the passage. You must discuss the effectiveness of your chosen features. Possible points include: literary and historical references reinforce perspective; inclusive personal language creates rapport; persuasive rhetorical techniques (repetition, questions, rhythms, etc.); urgent, compelling tone; dramatic images resonate.

Part (iii): remember, questions on the **visual** text require an analysis of both content and style. Begin by explicitly answering the question; for instance, *I would choose to project Image 2 and Image 3 as a backdrop to Mary Robinson as she delivered this speech . . .* Possible points include:

• Image 1: stark embodiment of Irish famine evokes sympathy; compelling artistic features (expression, colours, etc.); universal image of suffering is relevant and moving.

Discursive WRITING

- Image 2: reinforces the message 'to close the gap'; body language conveys genuine empathy; emphasises the importance of Mary Robinson's personal involvement.
- Image 3: graph amplifies meaning/<u>impact</u> of the speech; powerful and **emotive** headline and statistics command attention; dramatic and explicit representation of information.

Over to you: Make

Answer the following Leaving Certificate question using the tips and techniques below.

QUESTION B

Write **a proposal** to be submitted to the relevant authority (e.g. local council or national body), suggesting one event or person you believe should be commemorated. Explain why you feel this person or event should be commemorated and suggest what form this commemoration might take. (50)

Answer tips

There are a variety of approaches to writing a proposal, from the very formal to the personal. Choose an approach that suits you. You must, however, address all aspects of the task, though not necessarily equally. Take care to demonstrate the following:

- Clear appreciation of the task
- Consistency of **register**
- Effective reference/illustration
- Quality of your writing.

Techniques: Proposal

- Proposals are informative and persuasive writing because they attempt to educate the reader and to convince him or her to do something, in this case to commemorate a particular person.
- The goal of the writer is not only to persuade the reader to do what is being requested, but also to make him or her believe that the proposed solution is practical and appropriate.
- A proposal offers a plan: *what* you are proposing, *how* you plan to do it, *when* you plan to do it.
- The following general template for structuring reports can be adapted as required:

Introduction: Who do you propose should be commemorated?

↓

The **body**: Why should this person be commemorated?

↓

Conclusion: What form might this commemoration take?

Test yourself

This text is an extract from the script of *Good Night, and Good Luck,* a 2005 black-and-white film directed by George Clooney. It is based on real events that took place in the United States in the 1950s when CBS reporter Edward R. Murrow took a stand against Senator McCarthy's invasive investigation into people accused of having communist sympathies. In this opening extract Murrow is delivering a **speech** to fellow journalists.

from *Good Night, and Good Luck* by George Clooney and Grant Heslov

INTERIOR CHICAGO THEATER

October 15, 1958. The Radio and Television News Directors Association annual meeting.

We're in the wings of the theatre. Standing there alone is Edward R. Murrow. He looks slightly ill at ease. He lights a cigarette … he looks at some notes in his hand as we overhear his glowing introduction by the MC.

Cheers and applause as we walk with him to the podium.

A long awkward pause.

MURROW

This might just do nobody any good. At the end of this discourse a few people may accuse this reporter of fouling his own comfortable nest, and your organization may be accused of having given hospitality to heretical and even dangerous thoughts.

CUT TO:

Close ups of people listening. Smiling. Not aware that this is not to be the comfortable acceptance speech you might hear of a retiring employee getting his gold watch. This will become what will later be called "The Box of Lights and Wires Speech". One of THE MOST IMPORTANT broadcast journalism speeches EVER. It is an attack on everyone in this room … an attack on himself. And, at this point, it has just begun.

MURROW (CONT'D)

But the elaborate structure of Networks, Advertising Agencies and Sponsors will not be shaken or altered. It is my desire, if not my duty, to try to talk to you journeymen with some candor about what is happening to radio and television. If what I have to say is responsible, then I alone am responsible for the saying of it.

CUT TO:

MURROW

Our history will be what we make of it. And if there are any historians about fifty or a hundred years from now, and there should be preserved the Kinescopes for one week of all three networks, they will there find recorded in black and white, or color, evidence of decadence ... escapism, and insulation from the realities of the world in which we live. We are currently wealthy, fat, comfortable and complacent. We have a built-in allergy to unpleasant or disturbing information. Our mass media reflect this. But unless we get up off our fat surpluses and recognize that television in the main is being used to distract, delude, amuse and insulate us, then television and those who finance it, those who look at it and those who work at it, may see a totally different picture too late.

CUT TO:

Over black we read: **"The little picture"**

QUESTION A

(i) Based on your reading of the above text, what impression do you form of the speaker, Edward R. Murrow? Support your view with reference to the text. (15)

(ii) In 1958 Edward R. Murrow said that 'television in the main is being used to distract, delude, amuse and insulate us'. Do you think the same criticisms apply to the Internet today? Give reasons for your answer. (15)

(iii) Do you think this passage is a good example of effective speech-making? Give reasons for your answer. (20)

QUESTION B

(*from* Leaving Certificate Paper 1, Text 1, 2013)

You have been asked to give **a talk** to your class entitled 'Television and radio in the lives of young people today'. Write the text of the talk you would deliver in which you consider the role of television and radio in the lives of young people today. (50)

Discursive WRITING

Review and debate

Introduction

In this unit you will be introduced to reviews and debates, two different **genres** that have strong, opinionated argument as a common feature.

Reviews are a popular feature of many publications, such as newspapers, magazines and websites. A review is a summary and evaluation, most commonly of a book, a film or a music CD, but almost anything can be reviewed – an event, a restaurant, a home appliance. There are many professional reviewers, such as film critics and music journalists, but in recent years peer reviews have become very popular, especially on the Internet. Reading reviews prior to purchasing a product helps people to make decisions in a world that is full of choices.

A review should be relatively short with opinions delivered in a clear, <u>concise</u> manner. Factual material must be correct and a review should have a firm and assertive tone. The reviewer is entitled to whatever opinion he or she has, be it positive or negative, of the work or product, but that opinion must be substantiated with details and examples. The reviewer should establish a **register** – voice and personal style – that makes the review interesting. In addition to the critical evaluation, the reviewer may assign the work or product a rating to indicate its merit.

A **debate**, as we encounter it in English class, is a discussion – written or spoken – involving opposing points of view. A formal debate is a spoken contest of argumentation in which one team defends, and another team attacks, a given proposition. The winning team is usually chosen by neutral adjudicators according to a set of rules. Most contestants prepare for a debate by writing a **speech** and then practising its delivery. Impromptu debating requires contestants to 'think on their feet' and deliver points without a pre-prepared speech.

READ–ANALYSE–MAKE

The Lives of Others is a film directed by Florian Henckel von Donnersmarck. It explores the monitoring of people in East Berlin in the 1980s by the secret police. When it went on public release in the UK in 2007, the film was reviewed by Philip French in the *Observer*.

'Review of *The Lives of Others*' by Philip French

You know within minutes of watching *The Lives of Others*, the debut feature that brought writer-director Florian Henckel von Donnersmarck an Oscar for the best foreign language film of 2006, that you are in confident, authoritative hands. The film opens with an interrogation in East Berlin in 1984 at the temporary detention centre of the Ministry for State Security, better known as the Stasi. Forty years earlier, the Stasi's job was being done by the Gestapo, which was active for a mere dozen years and employed around 45,000 agents. The Stasi lasted 40 years in only half of the country, employed 100,000 full-time workers and had, so this movie tells us, 400,000 informants.

Woman peering through a gap in the Berlin Wall from West to East.

The interrogator in this initial scene is Captain Gerd Wiesler (Ulrich Muhe), a lean, humourless man seeking a confession from a political prisoner. There is no direct physical torture but the accused is made to sit on his hands and is forced to stay awake. Wiesler informs his victim that merely to question the probity of the Stasi is itself a serious crime.

When the necessary confession has been obtained, Wiesler places the fabric from the seat the prisoner has been sitting on in a bottle to retain the offender's odour for the use of tracker dogs. Wiesler then uses the tape recording of this scene to lecture recruits in the art of interrogation. While indoctrinating them in his form of mad logic, he's asked a question about the possible innocence of a victim; Wiesler puts a little cross beside the questioner's name. At the end of his lecture, he's buttonholed by a suspiciously hearty old school friend, Lieutenant-Colonel Anton Grubitz, now head of the Stasi's Cultural Department.

The sense of social unease and constant suspicion, which informs the whole of the film, leads on to the next scene: Grubitz takes Wiesler to the theatre and suggests he take an interest in a potentially dissident playwright, Georg Dreyman (Sebastian Koch), whose beautiful girlfriend (Martina Gedeck) is appearing in his new play. It is first hinted at, and then made clear, that an influential minister has designs on the actress and intends to use the Stasi to tarnish the playwright. Wiesler is assigned to the case by his old friend and proceeds to bug the writer's flat and put him under 24-hour surveillance.

We then see the Stasi at work, doggedly recording everything for the organisation's files, with entries in their log such as (noting the end of a birthday party) 'unwrap presents and then presumably have intercourse'. Their targets, however, are largely innocent of any plans to undermine the state. The theatre people are dedicated socialists who merely seek artistic freedom and a certain licence to criticise and exercise democratic rights.

Like Winston Smith in *Nineteen Eighty-Four*, the lonely, essentially decent Wiesler comes to doubt what he is doing and to suspect the patriotism of those around him. Listening in on the playwright and his girlfriend, he develops human sympathies and begins to make minor interventions, protecting the couple's privacy. He then acts in a serious, protective manner that puts his own life and career in danger.

The film turns into a suspenseful thriller with a complex and powerful moral drive. Were there people like Wiesler in the Stasi? Some of its victims say not. However, von Donnersmarck and Ulrich Muhe persuade us of that possibility without suggesting such figures were common.

The Lives of Others subtly evokes a vindictive society that exists by turning citizens against each other in the interests of national unity and collective security. It serves as a major warning to ourselves and our elected leaders about where overzealousness and a lack of respect for individuals and their liberties can lead.

The film has a remarkable coda, set in 1992 after the Berlin Wall has fallen and the Stasi files were opened to the public. When Dreyman the playwright visits the former Stasi headquarters, a trolley is required to bring in his bulky files. Reading them provides him with a walk down a nightmarish memory lane.

ANALYSE

Written text

Philip French's **review** of *The Lives of Others* is an excellent example of the **genre**. Film reviews are a mixture of informative writing, in which the reviewer tells us about the film, and argumentative writing, in which the reviewer presents an evaluation of the text. French succeeds admirably on both counts. In the first instance, he provides enough information about the plot of the film to engage the reader's interest, but not so much as to spoil the viewer's pleasure by telling the entire story. Ideally, a good film review, such as this one, should whet the reader's appetite to see the film for themselves.

As well as providing information, French offers the reader his evaluation, on a number of levels, of *The Lives of Others*. He applauds the convincing style of the film by praising the authority of the director. He compliments the content and the structure by demonstrating that the **narrative** of the film is an interesting one. He broadens the scope of his review and places the film within a wider cultural and artistic context through an **allusion** to another text, the novel *Nineteen Eighty-Four* by George Orwell, which also deals with totalitarian society and censorship. French identifies the genre of the film as 'a suspenseful thriller with a complex and powerful moral drive'. He asks a question about the text that has the effect of piquing the reader's curiosity: 'Were there people like Wiesler in the Stasi?' He comments on the relevance of the film to today's society – 'It serves as a major warning to ourselves and our elected leaders' – thereby further recommending it as an important work. Finally, in all aspects of his evaluation of *The Lives of Others*, he provides illustrations from the film to support his opinions, which is the signature of an excellent reviewer.

French's vocabulary and terminology throughout the review are drawn from the world of film. He refers, for instance, to the 'coda' of the film, a term given to a post-credits scene.

Visual text

The photograph depicts a section of the wall that divided the city of Berlin from 1961 to 1989. The wall dominates the **frame**, running as it does from east to west of the image. It is an imposing structure of large upright concrete blocks, bricks and planks of wood. Barbed wire, supported by metal poles, runs along the top of it. This image of the wall carries powerful connotations of prison and, in this particular historical context, of concentration camps.

In the background of the photo a block of high-rise flats is visible on the East German side of the wall. The building has all the hallmarks of the brutalist style of architecture that became synonymous with communist culture during this period. A large, windowless structure is also visible.

A concrete path can be seen in the foreground and central area of the photo.

To the left of the image a feature is partially visible. It appears to be a neglected flower bed, but it is not possible to be certain as most of the feature is outside the frame of the photo.

In the bottom right corner of the photo a woman is peering through a small chink in the wall. She is stooped and her hands are in the pockets of her coat. This tentative pose suggests a mixture of curiosity and trepidation. The woman, as the caption informs us, is from West Berlin, she is smartly dressed, which re-enforces the **contrast** between the two worlds divided by the wall.

The overall impression of the **visual** is of a joyless world – the lack of colour reinforces this, while the connotations of oppression, particularly in the image of the wall, create a sombre atmosphere.

Discursive WRITING

MAKE

QUESTION B

Imagine you are a journalist for an online magazine aimed at young people. Write **a website article** on the subject of 'Where overzealousness and a lack of respect for individuals and their liberties can lead'. (50)

Sample answer

First they came . . .

First they came for the socialists,
and I didn't speak out because I wasn't a socialist.
Then they came for the Jews,
and I didn't speak out because I wasn't a Jew.
Then they came for me,
and there was no one left to speak for me.

Home

About

News

Contacts

This quote is attributed to a German pastor and relates to the 'blind eye' that people turned to the treatment by the Nazis of particular groups such as socialists and Jews.

The quote is very powerful. It makes the point that if a society allows one group of people to be discriminated against or persecuted, then all groups within that society are vulnerable to the same treatment. I think this quote is as relevant today as it was in the 1930s, especially since we are now all citizens of the world and not just of one small country.

Today we take a lot for granted. We expect to be able to express our views, to be treated with respect, to make our own choices. This is as it should be. But we should not be complacent. Complacency, as history teaches us, threatens the very freedoms we take for granted.

I know people have a lot on their minds – peer pressure, economic recession, not to mention the dreaded Leaving Certificate – but it is necessary for us to be aware of where overzealousness and a lack of respect for individuals and their liberties can lead. Every time a private citizen's computer is hacked, or a person is arrested without due process, or a prisoner on hunger strike in Guantanamo Bay detention camp is force-fed, our freedom – the freedom we take for granted – is a little bit more vulnerable.

Gandhi, the man who brought independence to India through peaceful means, said that the strength of a society can be judged by how it treats its weakest members. These words are worth keeping in mind.

Advertisement for www.amnesty.org

Discursive WRITING

Techniques: Website article

- Layout is an important feature of Question B tasks. Organise your answer in imitation of the general layout of a website article; this may include: headline, subheading(s), **by-line**, links, side-bar.
- The **register** of a website article tends to be less formal than print articles and usually employs a relaxed, conversational tone.
- In a serious article such as the above, include evidence to support the points you make. This can be a mixture of soft evidence that illustrates the point (**anecdotes** and examples) and hard evidence that substantiates the point (facts, statistics and quotes).
- Use descriptive **imagery** to bring your article to life for the reader.
- Remember, in all journalistic texts the essential quality is clarity of expression.

Over to you: Read and analyse

As you read the following text from the 2009 Leaving Certificate exam paper, take note of the annotations in the margins and see if you can isolate the particular words and phrases that the annotations refer to. In this way you will improve your skills in both reading and analysing.

Text 1, 2009: Decisions for society

This text is taken from *Head to Head*, a series of public **debates**, published in April 2008 in *The Irish Times*; it consists of two extracts in response to the question:

Should Zoos be Closed?

NO, according to Veronica Chrisp (Head of Marketing at Dublin Zoo) who believes zoos connect us to the natural world.

Persuasive use of **emotive** *image*

Assertive tone and powerful **imagery** *combine to shift blame to those attacking zoos*

Short, concise, powerful statement

Expressive **adjective** *introduces sequence of* **metaphors** *relating to well-being*

If anybody could witness the look of amazement and wonder on the face of a six-year-old child as he, or she, sees an elephant, a snake or a gorilla for the very first time, it is unlikely that zoos would ever again be put on the defensive.

Of course, in our culture, the very word *zoo* has negative connotations – often evoking ideas of bored animals kept in Victorian menageries for the benefit of an unappreciative audience. Nothing could be further from the truth. Animals in zoos live enriched lives: they are fit and healthy, able to breed and raise their young. They can be observed in naturalistic spaces with vegetation and water features that reflect their native habitat and are designed with the animals' physical, psychological and social needs in mind. The designers of Dublin Zoo's Kaziranga forest trail, for example, sought inspiration

Use of **contrast** *to illustrate point*

Point supported by evidence

from the wild before ever setting pen to paper. Two healthy elephant calves later, the habitat is proving a delight for elephants and their visitors alike.

*Use of **concrete illustration** to support point*

The ethical and well-managed zoo has a vital role in our society: as a living classroom, conservation centre, animal sanctuary, centre of excellence in animal husbandry, science and research, and a major visitor attraction. And in order to remind people of the joy of the natural world, and to encourage and inspire visitors to understand wildlife, the zoo offers a really great day out for all.

List used to evidence point

*Persuasive use of **emotive** language*

Modern zoos are managed by caring professionals who devote their lives to the welfare of animals and to understanding their needs; they adhere to strict codes of practice in animal welfare laid down by European and global associations.

More than 900,000 people visited Dublin Zoo in 2007. All age groups, nationalities and different walks of life were represented – 50,000 of them were schoolchildren who visited as part of their formal education.

Factual evidence supports case

*Effective use of **rhetorical question** to evoke emotion*

Imagine the void left if the zoo was closed. Who would tell children about how elephants communicate, why monkeys hang by their tails or why flamingos are pink? How wonderful that they can see a real elephant or a zebra, or even a meerkat, without even having to switch on the television.

Forceful language

YES, according to Bernie Wright (Press Officer of the Alliance for Animal Rights) who believes zoos will always be prisons for animals.

Short, concise sentences create an authoritative tone

A zoo is simply a collection of animals. It makes money by attracting paying visitors. The quality of life for the animals varies from totally inadequate to barely adequate.

In 2008, Dublin Zoo sits on roughly 60 acres. It boasts such habitats as African plains, fringes of the Arctic, rainforests, the Kaziranga forest trail, and shops and restaurants. All of this, and 600 animals ranging from tigers, elephants and chimps to red pandas, hardly

Factual evidence

Discursive WRITING

Quotation from zoo is forcefully contested

seems like a natural environment. To quote the zoo, it invites visitors to "go wild in the heart of the city". It's a pity the animals cannot do the same. Indeed, it is well documented that elephants can roam more than 40 miles in a day in their natural surroundings.

*Effective use of **ironic** humour*

Strong attack on justification for zoos

Most animals on display in zoos are not threatened by extinction, yet captive breeding programmes which endeavour to save species are one of the most common reasons that zoos use to justify their existence. When asked how many animals have been reintroduced back into the wild by Dublin Zoo since the 1800s, the answer was "we have none in the records but possibly a golden lion tamarin". Strangely, there are no statistics for released animals.

Factual evidence

Effective use of quotation

Adverb used to intensify point

The focus of zoos is on human entertainment rather than education. They tend to be home to crowd-pleasers – animals that are cute, or massive, or funny, or ferocious. The Alliance for Animal Rights' observations show that even if learning material is available, most zoo-goers disregard it. Children, especially, rush from one exhibit to another, pausing only if animals are being fed or performing cute tricks. Good wildlife television programmes today can show normal behaviour of animals in their natural surrounds. Alternatively, there are safari jobs or holidays. We do not need to confine animals in zoos to learn.

Topic statement at beginning of section

Anecdotal evidence

Alternative options proposed

Some animals might live longer in zoos, but at what price? Elephants in captivity display chronic health problems. Other animals just go mad. Unnaturally housed or insane animals cannot be representative of their species. It is morally unacceptable to keep any being in an environment where natural instincts are continuously frustrated – the enclosure becomes a prison. I urge anyone who visits a zoo to really look into an animal's eyes. Do they deserve life imprisonment without ever committing a crime?

*Effective use of **rhetorical question***

Forceful language used to evoke emotion

*Prison **metaphor** effectively employed and extended in final rhetorical question*

Answer the following Leaving Certificate questions using the guidelines below.

QUESTION A

(i) Based on your reading of the above text, outline the views of Veronica Chrisp and Bernie Wright on **animal welfare in zoos**. (15)

(ii) Join the debate. Having considered the views expressed in the text, do **you** think zoos should be closed? Give reasons for your decision. (15)

(iii) Select **four features** of argumentative and/or persuasive writing evident in the text and comment on their effectiveness. Refer to the text in support of your answer. (20)

Discursive WRITING

Answer guidelines

Part (i): begin by explicitly answering the question; for instance, *From my reading of the text, I get a clear impression of the views of both Veronica Chrisp and Bernie Wright in relation to animal welfare in zoos.* Then outline the views of both writers (though not necessarily equally) on animal welfare in zoos. Possible points include:

- Veronica Chrisp: 'enriched lives' – physical, psychological, social; fit and healthy, able to raise young; 'naturalistic spaces', 'native habitat'; professional codes of practice.
- Bernie Wright: inadequate quality of life; confinement/imprisonment; health problems; natural instincts frustrated.

Part (ii): begin by answering the question; for instance, *Having considered the views expressed in the text, I do think zoos should/should not be closed.* As this is an opinion question, you are expected to make a decision and to develop a coherent viewpoint. You are free to anchor your reasons within the text or to use the text as a starting point for your argument. Possible points include: care and protection of animals; educational aspects; economic and tourism arguments; social and entertainment considerations; ill-treatment and exploitation of animals.

Part (iii): begin by answering the question; for instance, *There are many features of effective argumentative and/or persuasive writing evident in the text.* Then identify at least four features of style that make the text argumentative and/or persuasive. Remember, marks will be awarded for discussion of the effectiveness of your chosen features. Possible points include: interesting factual information to substantiate points; logical approach clarifies points; **anecdotal** evidence engages the reader; **emotive** language invigorates; rhetorical devices provoke.

Over to you: Make

Answer the following Leaving Certificate question using the tips and techniques below.

QUESTION B

'Go wild in the heart of the city'

Imagine you are making a cartoon film (featuring animals as characters) **either** to promote **or** to oppose zoos. Write **the script of a scene (in dialogue form)** between two of the animal characters. (50)

Answer tips

Present your chosen viewpoints in a drama script/**dialogue** format, and focus on the persuasive purpose of the task. The following features will be rewarded:

- Clear appreciation of the task
- Consistency of **register**
- Imaginative response
- Quality of your persuasive writing.

Discursive WRITING

Techniques: Drama script

A drama script is a written text designed for performance. Drama is different from novels and short stories because it is intended to be performed (on stage, radio or screen), which means it must sound authentic when read out loud. It also has to be presented in a special format.

A script consists of:

- **Dialogue** and **monologue** (what the characters say)
- Stage directions (instructions to the actors and director).

Here is an extract from the script of Brian Friel's stage drama *Dancing at Lughnasa*, which was first performed by the Abbey Theatre in 1990. Examine it carefully and note the special layout.

from *Dancing at Lughnasa*

The lighting changes. The kitchen and garden are now lit as for a warm summer evening.

MICHAEL, KATE, GERRY and FATHER JACK go off. The others busy themselves with their tasks.

CHRIS: D'you know what I think I might do? I think I just might start wearing lipstick.

AGNES: Do you hear this, Maggie?

MAGGIE: Steady on, girl. Today it's lipstick; tomorrow it's the gin bottle.

CHRIS: I think I just might.

AGNES: As long as Kate's not around. 'Do you want to make a pagan of yourself?'

(CHRIS puts her face up close to the mirror and feels it.)

CHRIS: Far too pale. And the aul mousey hair. Need a bit of colour.

AGNES: What for?

CHRIS: What indeed. *(She shrugs and goes back to her ironing. She holds up a surplice.)* Make a nice dress that, wouldn't it? . . . God forgive me . . .

(Work continues. Nobody speaks. Then suddenly and unexpectedly, ROSE bursts into raucous song:)

ROSE: 'Will you come to Abyssinia, will you come?

Bring your own cup and saucer and a bun . . .'

(As she sings the next two lines she dances – a gauche, graceless shuffle that defies the rhythm of the song.)

Notice the following features of the layout of a drama script:

- Title: in this case, *Dancing at Lughnasa.*
- Scene: where and when the scene is set: *kitchen and garden . . . warm summer evening.*
- Characters: say which characters are in the scene at the start: *The others busy themselves . . .* You should give any essential information; this might be their age, occupation or relationship with another character.

- Any characters who come into a scene after the start should be introduced by the word 'Enter' (for example: *Enter KATE*).
- Use 'Exit' when a character leaves.
- The name of the character who is speaking should be written at the left-hand side of the page. It is a good idea to print it in capitals. The name is followed by a colon (:), and then by the character's **dialogue**: *AGNES: What for?*
- Stage directions: instructions to the actors and director; these should be placed within brackets and underlined or italicised: *(Work continues. Nobody speaks . . .)*.

Test yourself

In August 2011 the *Guardian* newspaper asked its writers to pick their favourite albums ever. Here, Dave Simpson, a *Guardian* music critic, explains why Joy Division's *Closer* is one for all eternity.

'My Favourite Album' by Dave Simpson

Album cover with photograph of Appiani family tomb in Genoa, Italy

When I was still at school, I finished my Saturday job a couple of hours early to attend the first day of the Futurama festival in Leeds, headlined by Johnny Rotten's PiL, my first-ever gig. My mate and I had our photos taken in Woolies to put on the ticket. When we got there, punks sniffed glue outside while old ladies passed by, shrieking "Look at their hair!" I wore an iron-on Sid Vicious T-shirt. Everyone seemed much older and more knowing. We felt out of our depth and terrified.

Soon afterwards, Tony Wilson introduced "the awesome Joy Division". I remember singer Ian Curtis's hypnotically twitchy dancing and the way he seemed to be gazing over us at something troubling in the distance. Every time the crowd surged forward a skinhead's shoulder connected with my chin. By the end, I was in urgent need of a dentist but everything I'd previously thought about music had been turned on its head: it could be more than entertainment, more powerful than punk.

I soon bought the 'Transmission' single and then *Unknown Pleasures*, where Joy Division's raw power had been sculpted into science-fiction landscapes, with whirring lift shafts and slamming doors, by whizzkid producer Martin Hannett. My Dad had died when I was young, and I'd always been susceptible to songs with references to mortality such as Terry Jacks's 'Seasons in the Sun' and the Shangri-Las' 'The Leader of the Pack' – both made-up tales; there was something more real and troubling about Joy Division's 'New Dawn Fades'. What kind of 22-year old writes lyrics such as "a loaded gun, won't set you free"?

By the time their second album, *Closer*, was released only a few months later, Curtis had taken his own life. The clues were on the record, in 'Colony's "a cry for help, a hint of anaesthesia/ the sound from broken homes, we used to always meet here" and '24 Hours's "Destiny unfolded, I watched it slip away." It wasn't until much later – via Deborah Curtis's book and the *Control* film – that we were allowed the full, tragic details of Curtis's tailspin into worsening epilepsy, prescription drug-contributed depression and domestic turmoil. The Manchester band's hurtling journey had taken them from Warsaw – a proto-punk band who'd played Lou Reed covers and sported feather cuts and embarrassing moustaches – to 1980's stunning final album inside three years.

Back then, music was developing at a fast pace – disco towards rap and hip-hop; funk and reggae towards world music; punk into post-punk. *Closer* was a quantum leap from *Unknown Pleasures*, and sounded unlike anything else.

Guitar tracks such as 'Colony' and 'A Means to an End' sounded angular, brutal and unforgiving, almost chilling in their terrifying beauty. But then the deceptively perky 'Isolation' was mutated disco, which pointed the way towards electro-pop and the surviving members' regroup as New Order. '24 Hours', where Peter Hook's mournful bass intro leads into a guitar-raging whirlpool, is still the definitive Joy Division anthem.

Then there's the spectral serenity of the synthesiser tracks, truly emotional music made with machines. The whiplash drumbeat and haunting, sub-bass shadows of 'Heart and Soul'; the almost classical serenity of the piano-led, funereal 'The Eternal'; the awesome 'Decades', Curtis gazing sorrowfully at human suffering and warfare's "doors of hell's darker chambers", burdened by insights and events far beyond his years and his voice almost ghostly, a one-time punk with a new, Frank Sinatra-like croon.

It took three or four plays to fully hit home. But I can still remember an open window, the sun streaming on to my Fidelity UA4 stereo and a thought hitting me then that remains unchanged 31 years later: I love this album more than any music ever. For me, *Closer* contains the saddest, most beautiful music ever made.

QUESTION A

(i) In his review of both the concert and the album, how does Dave Simpson demonstrate that Joy Division deserve the description 'awesome'? Support your view with reference to the text. (15)

(ii) Both the written and visual elements of this text contain many striking images relating to mourning. Identify **three** such images that you find particularly striking and explain why you find them to be so. At least one of your chosen images must be the visual text. (15)

(iii) 'Reviews are a combination of informative and argumentative writing.' Identify **three** features of informative/argumentative writing in the above text and comment on their effectiveness. (20)

QUESTION B

Imagine that you are convinced you have discovered an unknown but talented band, singer or comedian. Write **an article for an entertainment website** in which you explain what is so impressive about the act, why the act should be promoted and why you think the act is going to be a major success. (50)

Article and report

Introduction

In this unit you will be introduced to two **genres** of writing that effectively and efficiently convey information: the article and the report.

An **article** is a written work published in a print or electronic medium and may include opinion so long as it is substantiated by evidence within the text. Most articles discuss news, current affairs and human interest stories, but articles can be written on almost any subject and may include photographs, accounts, statistics, interviews, polls and references. Quotations from various sources are particularly helpful in confirming the factuality and reliability of the writer's information.

Articles are generally structured as follows:

- Headline: text at the top of an article, indicating the nature of the article. The headline catches the attention of the reader and relates well to the topic.
- **By-line**: gives the name and often the role of the writer, such as foreign affairs correspondent or chief sports writer.
- Lead: sentence that captures the attention of the reader and introduces the focus of the article. The lead also establishes the subject, sets the tone and guides the reader into the text.

A **report** is a document made with the specific intention of relaying information in a presentable form. A report may also offer assessments or recommendations on the basis of the information provided. One of the most common formats for presenting reports is:

IMRAD: **I**ntroduction, **M**ethods, **R**esults **A**nd **D**iscussion

Additional elements found in reports include headings, charts, tables, figures, pictures and references. Reports fill a vast array of critical needs for many organisations, including governments, banks and schools. The information contained in some reports, such as those issued by the Central Statistics Office, may be used to make important decisions that affect our lives.

Discursive WRITING

As well as reports, informative texts include journalism (newspaper, television and radio), instructions, memos, letters, summaries, bulletins, forms and questionnaires. These informative texts have particular and varying objectives, but they all exhibit the following common features:

- Clear organisation of information
- Logical structure and layout
- Relevant and succinct content
- Simple, factual language
- Short sentences
- **Objective** tone.

READ–ANALYSE–MAKE

On 11 September 2001, often referred to as 9/11, militants associated with the Islamic extremist group al-Qaeda hijacked four airliners and carried out suicide attacks against targets in the United States. Two of the planes were flown into the towers of the World Trade Center in New York City. The following is the adapted text of an article published in the *Guardian* in 2011.

Discursive WRITING

READ

'The Meaning of 9/11's Most Controversial Photo' by Jonathan Jones

In the photograph Thomas Hoepker took on 11 September 2001, a group of New Yorkers sit chatting in the sun in a park in Brooklyn. Behind them, across brilliant blue water, in an azure sky, a terrible cloud of smoke and dust rises above lower Manhattan from the place where two towers were struck by hijacked airliners this same morning and have collapsed, killing, by fire, smoke, falling or jumping or crushing and tearing and fragmentation in the buildings' final fall, nearly 3,000 people.

Ten years on, this is becoming one of the iconic photographs of 9/11, yet its history is strange and tortuous. Hoepker, a senior figure in the renowned Magnum photographers' co-operative, chose not to publish it in 2001 and to exclude it from a book of Magnum pictures of that horribly unequalled day. Only in 2006, on the fifth anniversary of the attacks, did it appear in a book, and then it caused instant controversy. The columnist Frank Rich wrote about it in the *New York Times*. He saw in this undeniably troubling picture an allegory of America's failure to learn any deep lessons from that tragic day, to change or reform as a nation: "The young people in Mr Hoepker's photo aren't necessarily callous, they're just American."

In other words, in a country that believes in moving on they have already moved on, enjoying the sun in spite of the scene of mass carnage that scars the fine day.

Rich's view of the picture was instantly disputed. Walter Sipser, identifying himself as the guy in shades at the right of the picture, said he and his girlfriend, apparently sunbathing on a wall, were in fact "in a profound state of shock and disbelief". Hoepker, they both complained, had photographed them without permission in a way that misrepresented their feelings and behaviour.

Well, you can't photograph a feeling. But another five years on since it surfaced in 2006, it seems pointless to argue about the morality of the people in the picture, or of the photographer, or his decision to withhold the picture from publication. It is now established as one of the defining images of that day as it is the only photograph to assert the art of the photographer: among hundreds of devastating pictures, by amateurs as well as professionals, that horrify and transfix us because they record the details of a crime that outstripped imagination, this one stands out as a more ironic, distanced, and therefore artful, image. Perhaps the real reason Hoepker sat on it at the time was because it would be egotistical to assert his own cunning as an artist in the midst of mass slaughter.

Today, the meaning of this photograph has nothing to do with judging individuals. It has become a picture about history, and about memory. As an image of a cataclysmic historical moment it captures something that is true of all historical moments: life does not stop dead because a battle or an act of terror is happening nearby.

History is not a heroic story, nor memory a block of marble inscribed with imperishable words of grief and rage. As Tony Blair says of that day in his book *A Journey*, "It is amazing how quickly shock is absorbed and the natural rhythm of the human spirit reasserts itself . . . We remember, but not as we felt at that moment."

The meaning of this photograph is that memories fade fast. The people in the foreground are us. We are the ones whose lives went on, touched yet untouched, separated from the heart of the tragedy by the blue water of time, which has got ever wider and more impossible to cross. A past event belongs to history, not the present. To feel the full sorrow of it now you need to watch a documentary – and then you will switch to something lighter, either because it is painfully clear that too much blood has been spent around the world in the name of this disaster, or simply because changing channels is what humans do. The people in this photograph cannot help being alive, and showing it.

ANALYSE

Discursive WRITING

Written text

This text by Jonathan Jones is an opinion article. Its purpose is explicitly stated in the heading: 'The Meaning of 9/11's Most Controversial Photo' – and the article then proceeds to outline the writer's view. Jones begins by providing a vivid description of the photograph. He employs strong **visual imagery** to highlight the **contrast** inherent in the photo: a group of young people 'chatting in the sun in a park in Brooklyn' while behind them 'a terrible cloud of smoke and dust rises above lower Manhattan'. The opening paragraph succeeds in both capturing the attention of the reader and introducing the focus of the article.

Jones takes a logical approach to outlining his views on the controversial photo. Having described the photo in the opening paragraph, and drawn attention to the disturbing **juxtaposition** of images within it, he now turns his attention to the history of the photo. Factual evidence is employed to inform the reader of its history and a quotation is used to illustrate the views of the columnist Frank Rich with regard to the photo. Throughout this section, even though he is conveying factual information, Jones continues to use forceful language, as befits the subject matter he is discussing: 'that horribly unequalled day'.

In keeping with a balanced article, Jones includes a viewpoint that counters the one expounded by Frank Rich. He tells us that Walter Sipser, 'identifying himself as the guy in shades at the right of the picture', disputes Rich's interpretation of the photo. This information provides balance in the article, an essential ingredient in good journalism.

Having provided the reader with a clear overview of both the history of the photo and the conflicting analyses it has inspired, Jones now proceeds to offer his own reading of the contentious image. His point, that 'it is the only photograph to assert the art of the photographer', is delivered with lucidity and force. In this section of the article Jones makes a number of similarly assertive points – for example, 'History is not a heroic story' – but he always offers evidence in the form of quotations and illustration to substantiate these. This approach is vital in good journalism.

A strong tone is employed in the conclusion of the article. Jones uses **metaphor** in an **emotive** way, relating it closely to the visual text: 'the blue water of time'. He also encourages our receptive response to the article by addressing us as 'We' and 'You'. The use of both first person plural and second person **pronouns** has the effect of drawing the reader into the text and setting up an intimate relationship between the reader and the writer of the article. Finally, the article ends with what most people would consider a truism: 'changing channels is what humans do'. This is the hallmark of particularly good article writing.

Visual text

In the background of the photograph a distant grey cityscape extends across the horizon. A massive plume of black smoke engulfs the buildings in the centre and extends upwards into the blue sky.

In the foreground a group of five people sit in a loosely formed circle. Their body language is relaxed – one figure squats, another leans back as though to catch the conversation, the three others sit hunched with their elbows on their knees. The casual clothing and demeanour of the people, along with the bicycle parked in the centre of the group, suggest leisure.

The people are neatly framed by two green yew trees, one to the left of them and one to the right, which run the length of the **visual**.

At the centre of the image is a large expanse of blue water. In the context of the photo, it serves as a **metaphor** for distance, since the carnage in the background and the seemingly relaxed interaction of the people in the foreground are, in this image, shockingly juxtaposed.

Discursive WRITING

MAKE

QUESTION B

Imagine that you have set up a club in your school to promote the visual arts. Write **the information leaflet** you would use to promote your club within the school. (50)

Sample answer

> **The VAC**
>
> **St Brendan's Visual Arts Club**
>
> *Insert visual here - iconic movie poster such as Casablanca or The Third Man*

What is it?	The VAC – the Visual Arts Club – is a club for people who are interested in film, sculpture, photography or any visual art form. It is a chance to get together with like-minded individuals and have some fun discussing, viewing and learning more about your favourite films and works of visual art.
Who is it for?	The VAC is for you. Any age, any gender, any species (well nearly!) is welcome to join the VAC. The VAC is fun, but you will also learn loads. The VAC is perfect for anyone thinking of a future career in media, film, language, or anyone generally interested in the visual arts.
When is it on?	The VAC takes place every Friday after school in the library from 4 to 6 p.m. (approx.). The only (really strict) rule is no eating or drinking in the library.
Why should I go?	Have you ever watched a film and thought *What's that all about?* (Come on, we've all seen *Donnie Darko* . . .)
	OR looked at artwork in a book, gallery or public space and thought *What does it mean?* (What about *all* modern art?)
	OR wondered what it was about a particular photograph that made it so memorable?
	If so, then the VAC is for you.
	Find out what words like homage, chiaroscuro and intertextuality actually mean. Meet new friends – and some old ones. Come along to the library on Friday afternoons to watch films, take part in discussions, make presentations, listen to guest speakers, compete in quizzes and much, much more.
	The VAC, as a famous actor once said, is *the stuff that dreams are made of*.

Insert logo here – letters 'V', 'A' and 'C' in a movie projector beam

For further information contact Niall Nugent at artsclub@stbrendans.ie

Discursive WRITING

Techniques: Information leaflet

- Leaflets are printed sheets of paper that provide information.
- Layout should include some or all of the following: heading, subheading(s), **visual**(s), logo, bullet points, table(s).
- Content should include some or all of the following: <u>concise</u>, factual information; imperatives (forceful, commanding language); quotations and/or statistics; direct appeal to the reader; contact details.

Over to you: Read and analyse

As you read the following text from the 2013 Leaving Certificate exam paper, take note of the annotations in the margins and see if you can isolate the particular words and phrases that the annotations refer to. In this way you will improve your skills in both reading and analysing.

Text 3, 2013: Story-telling

This edited text is based on an article from *The Irish Times* by Belinda McKeon entitled: 'New York Stories on a Perfect Platform'. It celebrates the hundredth anniversary of the opening of New York's Grand Central Station.

For many New Yorkers, it was the photographs of an evacuated Grand Central Station that drove home the realisation that Hurricane Sandy was on its way. Without people on its marble concourse, the city's huge rail terminal was a place that looked, somehow, lost. It was never meant to be empty. It was designed not just to be full of people but to be given form by people; it was not one of those architectural marvels whose creator secretly wished that visitors would stay away and leave it to its perfection of proportion and line. The vision of Grand Central's chief architect, Whitney Warren, was for a terminal that would be all about the crowd. Turn-of-the-century New York was a human <u>maelstrom</u>, teeming and diverse; Warren sought to offer a more ordered idea of urban existence. What had been an unpredictable stampede elsewhere in the city became, in Warren's carefully engineered spaces, a graceful dance. The passengers wove their way around the concourse, they people-watched from the galleries and they gazed up to the ceiling, arching high overhead, painted with all the stars and signs of the zodiac. It was a seemingly spontaneous choreography.

Variety of sentence lengths

Metaphor creates vivid image

*Use of **personification** gives character to the station*

Factual information woven into the text

Hyperbole used to emphasise point

Metaphor is extended for effect

Unsurprisingly, this daily dance of spectacle and observation has proven irresistible for photographers and film-makers over the years. Perhaps the most <u>iconic</u> images of Grand Central are the black-and-white shots by John Collier. They show the concourse <u>pinioned</u> by great shafts of sunlight. Who wouldn't want to turn a camera on the place? Whether you push in from 42nd Street or

Effective use of question

Discursive WRITING

Effective use of verbs trudge up from the grime and <u>ruckus</u> of the subway, the sight of Grand Central's concourse does something to the soul.

Reportage of announcement creates a realistic atmosphere

And the sounds: the call to the trains, the spry voice of the announcer seeming as though it's addressed to you alone: "Your 4.45 to Poughkeepsie is now on track 102." The inimitable echo: 1,000 footsteps on marble every minute of every day. After all, there are the stories of a city, and there are the stories that a city tells itself about itself, and in many ways Grand Central has been one of those stories. Fiction set there is often the fiction of characters who are unable to see certain realities; who are dazzled by the glow of the things in which they fervently want to believe.

Auditory imagery brings station to life

Effective use of simile

So John Cheever's teenage narrator in *Reunion* (1962) arranges to meet his estranged father here; his young hopes, stacked as high as the vaulted ceiling, can only go one way. In another Cheever story, *O City of Broken Dreams* (1948), the Malloy family come to New York in search of fame; as she steps off the train, Alice wonders if the "frosty glitter" of the platform is the dust of trodden diamonds.

Allusion used as evidence to support earlier point

The passengers on the concourse are tiny figures in relation to the scale of the building, suggesting the position of humanity in the universe

Black-and-white photography creates a classic, timeless image

The vast height of the roof and the arched windows give the impression of a cathedral; coupled with the streaming shafts of light, this creates an almost religious atmosphere

Image 1: John Collier's <u>iconic</u> photograph of the concourse of Grand Central Station

In the early Richard Yates' story *A Glutton for Punishment*, a businessman readying for a date uses a "gleaming <u>subterranean</u> dressing room" at Grand Central; washed, shaved and with his suit pressed, he emerges a more polished version of his usual self, but also a little poorer, for in the heady gladness of it all he has tipped the attendant more than he can afford. If there is a poet of Grand Central, it must be Yates, whose novels and stories are born out of the very tension between that place's everyday treadmill and its <u>gilded</u> promises.

Contrast used effectively

Discursive WRITING

And in homage to Cheever, Richard Ford's story *Reunions* (2000) is another study in self-delusion at Grand Central, an account of a wrong-headed attempt at reconciliation, during which the narrator allows himself to be unwisely reassured by the "eddying currents" of the crowd. "I had been wrong," he chides himself at the story's end, "about the linkage of moments." Because, in Grand Central, we may all of us seem linked for a moment, but who knows what is really going on in any one of those glimpsed lives?

Quotations used to illustrate tone of the story

Effective use of question to provoke a response in reader

The last time I passed through the terminal was on a Friday in December, going to the Bronx for the funeral of my husband's uncle. As we headed for our track, the arriving trainloads from Connecticut were spilling out on to the concourse, weaving themselves into its choreography, doing their steps of that every-morning dance. It was 9.15 a.m. Hours later, as news too horrific to countenance came out of a Connecticut school, on the train back to Grand Central that evening, a young woman opposite me read something on her phone, and her face twisted with sorrow. Our eyes met and I shook my head – I didn't need a translation – and she shook hers.

Anecdote used to personalise point

Dance metaphor employed once more

Effective visual image

In the Biltmore Room, an old chalkboard schedule lists the cross-country trains that once arrived at 42nd Street: the Knickerbocker, the Missourian, the 20th Century Limited. Once known as the Kissing Room because of the many welcomes bestowed here, not least upon returning troops, this space houses little activity now, apart from some shoe-shining and newspaper-buying. Still, there's a nook here that is perhaps my favourite of all in Grand Central: the little windowed booth where the dozens of pairs of shoes resoled by Eddie's Shoe Repair sit, in their brown paper bags, all fixed up and ready to go. Ready to echo across that marble again.

Factual detail

Effective use of circular structure: the text ends with an image that mirrors its opening

Concrete details add realism to the text

The station appears as a huge gallery full of diminutive people, perhaps suggesting the fleeting nature of existence when compared with the immortality of art

The image's rich, autumnal colour palette evokes a strong sense of the passage of time

Image 2: The concourse of Grand Central Station

Answer the following Leaving Certificate questions using the guidelines below.

QUESTION A

(i) What evidence does the writer offer to suggest that Grand Central Station has gripped people's imaginations since its opening in 1913? Support your answer with reference to the written text. (15)

(ii) Both the written and visual elements of Text 3 contain many striking images that capture the grandeur and atmosphere of Grand Central Station. Identify **three** images that you find particularly striking and explain why you find them to be so. The images may be taken solely from the written text or from a combination of the written and visual texts. (15)

(iii) In the above extract, Belinda McKeon effectively communicates both knowledge of, and affection for, Grand Central Station. Discuss this statement with reference to both the content and style of the written text. (20)

Answer guidelines

Part (i): begin by explicitly answering the question; for instance, *The writer offers a great deal of evidence to suggest that Grand Central Station has gripped people's imaginations since its opening in 1913*. Then outline at least three pieces of evidence presented by Belinda McKeon in the text. Possible points include: passengers 'people-watched from the galleries' and 'gazed up to the ceiling'; 'irresistible for photographers and film-makers over the years'; Grand Central has been the setting for many fictional stories; the station inspires 'the stories that a city tells itself about itself'; the writer's own imagination is gripped by the station.

Part (ii): begin by answering the question; for instance, *Both the written and visual elements of Text 3 contain many striking images that capture the grandeur and atmosphere of Grand Central Station*. Then identify three images and explain in detail why you find them to be particularly striking. Possible points include:

- Visual image 1: the vastness of the station in relation to the passengers and the almost heavenly shafts of light suggest the position of humanity in the universe and the grandeur of Grand Central. Black-and-white photography and shafts of light capture an almost mystical atmosphere.

- Visual image 2: the station appears as a huge gallery full of diminutive people, perhaps suggesting the fleeting nature of existence in comparison with the immortality of art. The rich autumnal palette of colours captures a magical atmosphere.

- Written text: recurring **metaphor** of dance woven throughout the text to illustrate the movement of passengers within the station. Memorable **auditory** images such as the 'inimitable echo: 1,000 footsteps on marble every minute of every day' suggest the bustling, magical atmosphere. Specific images of grandeur used throughout the text: 'huge rail terminal', 'all the stars and signs of the zodiac', 'pinioned by great shafts of sunlight'.

Part (iii): begin by answering the question; for instance, *In the extract, Belinda McKeon effectively communicates both knowledge of, and affection for, Grand Central Station.* Then discuss this statement with reference to both the content and style of the written text. Possible points include:

- Knowledge: factual information (content); literary **allusion** (content); personal experience (content).

- Affection: **rhetorical questions** expressing awe and admiration (style): 'Who wouldn't want to turn a camera on the place?'; personal tone expressive of warm feelings (style): 'Still, there's a nook here that is perhaps my favourite of all'; striking **imagery** suggesting pleasure (style): 'spontaneous choreography'.

Over to you: Make

Answer the following Leaving Certificate question using the tips and techniques below.

QUESTION B

Write **an opinion piece**, for inclusion in a series of newspaper articles entitled *Must-see Attractions for Tourists*, in which you identify **one** place **or** public building in Ireland that, in your opinion, tourists should visit and explain your choice. (50)

Answer tips

The opinion piece must be suitable for publication in a newspaper. Use the series heading: *Must-see Attractions for Tourists*. Clearly identify your choice of place or public building and explain in detail why tourists should visit there. The following features will be rewarded:

- Clear appreciation of the task
- Consistency of **register**
- Imaginative response
- Quality of your persuasive language.

Techniques: Opinion piece

- Organise your answer in imitation of the general layout of an opinion piece in a newspaper: headline, subheading, **by-line**, reasonably short paragraphs.
- Choose your **register** to suit the style of an opinion piece: a mixture of personal, persuasive, informative, discursive, humorous and so on.
- Include descriptive **imagery** to bring your piece to life for the reader.
- Remember, in all journalistic texts the essential quality is clarity of expression.

Test yourself

Every year the Central Statistics Office (CSO) in Ireland produces a report entitled *Women and Men in Ireland*, in which trends in terms of differences and similarities between the genders are recorded. The text below is adapted from the CSO press release offering an overview of the 2011 report.

Discursive WRiTiNG

Press release: *Women and Men in Ireland 2011* (CSO)

Women are more likely to have a third-level qualification than men. Over half of women aged between 25 and 35 have a third-level qualification compared with less than four out of ten men. Boys are more likely to leave school early, and girls do better than boys at second level. These facts are contained in the report *Women and Men in Ireland 2011* published by the CSO.

Education: The early school leavers rate among women aged 18–24 in 2010 was 8.4%, which was much lower than the male rate of 12.6%. In 2011 more girls obtained an A or B on the honours paper in the Leaving Certificate exams in English, Irish, French, Biology, Chemistry, Art and Music while more boys obtained an A or B on the honours paper in Maths, Physics, Construction studies and Engineering. Women are more likely to have a third-level qualification, with over half (53%) of women aged 25–34 having a third-level qualification compared with nearly four out of ten men (39%) in this age group.

Employment: The employment rate for men in Ireland stood at about 75% over recent years, but in 2009 it plummeted to 67.3%, decreased sharply in 2010 to 64.5% and dropped again to 63.3% in 2011. The EU target rate for women in employment is 60% (2010), a target that was met by Ireland in 2007 and 2008, but not in 2009, 2010 or 2011, when the rate had fallen to 56%.

Decision-making: The report shows that women are under-represented in decision-making structures at both national and regional levels. In 2011, only 15.1% of TDs in Dáil Éireann were women. The average representation in national parliaments for EU countries was nearly a quarter in 2011.

Population: The highest fertility rate in the EU in 2010 was in Ireland at 2.07, well above the EU average of 1.59. The average age at which women gave birth to their first child rose from 25 years in 1980 to 29.4 years in 2010. Ireland had 98 men per 100 women in the population in 2011. This masks differences in the age groups: at younger ages, there are more boys than girls (as more boys are born than girls), there are fewer men than women in the 20–29 age group as more males than females have emigrated in recent years, and at older ages, there are more women than men (as women live longer than men).

Migration: Emigration rose steeply between 2006 and 2011 to about 38,700 males and 37,800 females, resulting in a net outflow leaving the country in 2011 of 18,600 males and 15,500 females.

Health: Women were more likely to be hospitalised in 2010, with 343 hospital discharges per 1,000 women compared with 305 discharges per 1,000 men. Men are more likely to be admitted to psychiatric hospitals for schizophrenia and alcoholic disorders while women are more likely to be admitted for depression.

Economic sectors: In primary education, 85% of teachers are women. And in second-level education, 63% of teachers are women. Despite this, women are not well represented at senior level positions: only 36% of medical and dental consultants are women, 53% of primary school managers, and 41% of second-level school managers.

Income: The report shows that women's income in 2009 was around 73% of men's income. After adjusting for the longer hours worked by men, women's hourly earnings were around 94% of men's.

Poverty: The proportion of men at risk of poverty in 2010, after pensions and social transfers, was 15%, just above the rate of 14% for women. At risk of poverty rates were considerably lower for those in employment, at 10% for men and 5% for women.

Crime: There were 12,487 persons committed to prison under sentence in 2010, of whom one in eight was female. 47 men and 11 women were victims of murder/manslaughter in 2010.

QUESTION A

(i)   In your opinion, what are the **three** most interesting revelations in the above press release? Give reasons for your answer and support your view with reference to the text. (15)

(ii) You have been asked to make recommendations to the Irish government on the basis of the findings contained in the report *Men and Women in Ireland 2011.* In relation to **two** of the following areas – education, decision-making, economic sectors – write out the recommendations that you would make. (15)

(iii) In your opinion, what features of an effective report are evident in the above text? Give reasons for your answer and support your view with reference to the text. (20)

QUESTION B

You have been asked by your school principal to write **an information leaflet** on Diversity Week in your school. It should focus on the activities organised by various groups within the school, and promote awareness among students of the issues surrounding discrimination against minority groups. (50)

Discursive essay

Introduction

The **discursive essay** is one of the main composition types set on the Leaving Certificate paper.

In the discursive essay you are invited to express your views and opinions on a particular subject. This is analytical writing in which points are made and arguments are constructed. Evidence, descriptive detail and persuasive techniques are used to convince the reader and keep your composition interesting. Discussion essays can be light-hearted and informal or serious and formal, but they always follow a logical structure.

Open your essay with a **hook** – a paragraph designed to draw the reader in and make him or her want to continue reading your essay. The tone of the hook should be consistent with the approach of the entire essay (formal or informal) and it should lead in to your central argument or main point. The most popular hooks are personal **anecdote**, **dialogue** and description.

The next section is your introduction to the topic of the essay. It should explicitly address the title and briefly outline the points that you intend to develop in your essay.

The **body** of the essay consists of a series of paragraphs (three or more), each addressing a particular point in relation to the title of the essay. Evidence should be used to support your points. Remember that soft evidence consists largely of anecdotes and examples, whereas hard evidence incorporates facts, statistics, quotations and so on. Soft evidence is employed more in light-hearted, informal texts and generally used to illustrate a point; hard evidence is more suited to serious, formal texts and to proving a point. Most discursive texts make use of both types of evidence.

It is essential to keep your writing lively by employing descriptive detail and persuasive techniques. Descriptive detail includes vivid **imagery** and the effective use of **simile** and/or **metaphor**. Persuasive techniques include **rhetorical questions**, **triadic structures**, forceful language, **exhortation**, repetition, exaggeration for effect and **ironic** humour.

The conclusion of a discursive essay should offer a brief summary of the main points that you have made. However, don't end merely with this summary. It is a nice touch to bring your essay to a close with the use of **circular structure**, whereby you return to the subject of your opening hook and reference it once more. The use of this technique creates circularity in the structure of your essay since you begin and end with the same subject matter.

Discursive WRITING

Techniques: Discursive essay

The most popular types of discursive essay on the Leaving Certificate paper are **speeches**, **talks** and articles. Remember, while different types of discursive essay have different forms, they all comply with the structure outlined above.

Writing speeches or talks

- Speeches are always for or against a topic or motion, whereas talks can discuss all sides of a subject.

- Employ a suitable address. A speech usually has a formal opening: *Ladies and gentlemen*. A **debate** speech often begins: *Chairperson, adjudicators, members of the proposition/opposition, ladies and gentlemen.* A talk has a more relaxed opening, suited to the audience being addressed; for example: *Fellow classmates*.

- Employ an appropriate **register** in your speech or talk. Talks are generally less formal; speeches are always formal.

- Connect with your audience. Use a **hook** to draw the audience in – an **anecdote**, **concrete illustration** or description of a person or place usually works well.

- Use clear, coherent language and vary the length of sentences.

- Employ evidence – mainly soft evidence (anecdote and examples) in talks, and mainly hard evidence (facts, statistics, quotes of experts) in speeches.

- Tone is very important in speeches and talks. A conversational tone creates a relaxed atmosphere between speaker and audience, whereas a more forceful or **didactic** tone is effective in persuading an audience towards a particular viewpoint.

- Use persuasive devices and descriptive detail to convince your audience and keep your speech or talk interesting.

- Persuasive devices include **contrast**, **triadic structure**, **exhortation**, repetition, **rhetorical questions** and forceful language.

Additional points for writing articles and essays

- Draw the reader into your text by employing an interesting **hook**.

- Although your article or essay is focused on a particular topic, remember that you may adopt an explicit or implicit approach. An explicit approach sets out the argument at the outset of the text, whereas an implicit approach makes the argument later in the text after evidence has been used to draw the reader in.

- Depending on the **register** of the article or essay you are writing, you may adopt either an **objective** or a **subjective** approach.

READ–ANALYSE–MAKE: Discursive Essay One

Bill Bryson is a best-selling American author of humorous books on travel, as well as books on the English language and on science. The following extract is from Chapter 14, 'The Hard Sell',

Discursive WRITING

of *Made in America*, a non-fiction book describing the history of the English language in the United States and the evolution of American culture.

from *Made in America* by Bill Bryson

On 1 July 1941 the New York television station WNBT-TV interrupted its normal viewing to show, without comment, a Bulova watch ticking. For sixty seconds the watch ticked away mysteriously, then the picture faded and normal programming resumed. It wasn't much, but it was the first television commercial.

Both the word and the idea were already established. The first *commercial* – the word used from the very beginning – had been broadcast by radio station WEAF in New York on 28 August 1922. It lasted for either ten or fifteen minutes, depending on which source you credit. Commercial radio was not an immediate hit but, by the mid-1920s, sponsors were not only flocking to buy air-time but naming their programmes after their products – *The Lucky Strike Hour* and so on. Such was the <u>obsequiousness</u> of the radio networks that by the early 1930s many were allowing the sponsors to take complete artistic and production control of the programmes. Many of the more popular shows were actually written by the advertising agencies, and the agencies seldom missed an opportunity to work a favourable mention of the sponsor's products into the scripts.

With the rise of television in the 1950s, the practises of the radio era were effortlessly transferred to the new medium. Advertisers inserted their names into the programme title – *Texaco Star Theater*, *Gillette Cavalcade of Sports*, *The Ford Star Jubilee*. Sponsors didn't write the programmes any longer, but they did impose a firm control on the contents, most notoriously during a 1959 *Playhouse* broadcast of *Judgement at Nuremburg*, when the sponsor, the American Gas Association, managed to have all references to gas ovens and the gassing of Jews removed from the script.

Where commercial products of the late 1940s had scientific-sounding names, those of the 1950s relied increasingly on secret ingredients. Gleem toothpaste contained a mysterious piece of alchemy called GL-70. Consumers were never given the slightest hint of what GL-70 was, but it would, according to the advertising, not only rout odour-causing bacteria but 'wipe out their enzymes!'*

A kind of creepy illiteracy invaded advertising too, to the dismay of many. When Winston began advertising its cigarettes with the slogan 'Winston tastes good like a cigarette should', columnists wrote anguished essays on what the world was coming to – every educated person knew it should be '*as* a cigarette should' – but the die was cast. By 1958 Ford was advertising that you could 'travel smooth' in a Thunderbird Sunliner and the maker of Ace Combs was urging buyers to 'comb it handsome' – a trend that continues today with 'pantihose that fits you real comfortable' and other grammatical manglings too numerous and too dispiriting to dwell on.

We may smile at the advertising ruses of the 1920s – frightening people with the threat of 'fallen stomach' and 'scabby toes' – but in fact such creative manipulation still goes on. When Kentucky Fried Chicken introduced 'Extra Crispy' chicken to sell alongside its 'Original' chicken, and sold it at the same price, sales were disappointing. But when its advertising agency persuaded it to promote 'Extra Crispy' as a premium brand and to put the price up, sales soared. Truth has seldom been a particularly visible feature of American advertising.

In <u>linguistic</u> terms, perhaps the most interesting challenge facing advertisers today is that of selling products in an increasingly multicultural society. Spanish is a particular problem, not just because it is spoken over such a widely scattered area but also because it is spoken in so many different forms. Brown sugar is *azucar negra* in New York, *azucar prieta* in Miami, *azucar morena* in much of Texas, and *azucar pardo* pretty much everywhere else – and that's just one word. Much the same bewildering multiplicity applies to many others. In consequence, embarrassments are all but inevitable. In mainstream Spanish *bichos* means *insects*, but in Puerto Rico it means *testicles*, so when a pesticide maker promised to bring death to the *bichos* Puerto Rican consumers were at least bemused, if not alarmed.

Never mind. Sales soared.

* For purposes of research, I wrote to Procter & Gamble, Gleem's manufacturer, asking what GL-70 was, but the public relations department, evidently thought it eccentric of me to wonder what I had been putting in my mouth all through childhood and declined to reply.

Discursive WRITING

ANALYSE

This extract is an excellent example of a light-hearted and humorous discursive text. Bryson's **hook** in the opening paragraph is an account of the first television advertisement, which is effective in both arousing the reader's interest and introducing the subject of the text: advertising.

The structural development of the text is logical. Following the hook, each paragraph discusses a particular point related to the subject of advertising: radio, TV, secret ingredients, the language of advertising, creative manipulation and the challenge of selling products in a multicultural society. The piece has a **circular structure**: its concluding 'Sales soared' is an obvious link back to 'commercial' in the opening paragraph; both highlight the essential purpose of advertising, which is to make money.

The text is written in a style that is lively and engaging. To a large extent this is due to the colourful and wide-ranging evidence employed to illustrate the points being made. Bryson uses a number of interesting factual examples in support of his views – *The Lucky Strike Hour*, for instance – but he also provides enjoyable **anecdotes** to enhance the personal tone: 'what I had been putting in my mouth all through childhood'.

The use of persuasive devices also adds interest to the text. **Colloquial** language, such as 'creepy illiteracy', appeals to the reader and the <u>wry</u> tone employed throughout creates a gentle, mocking humour: 'Puerto Rican consumers were at least bemused, if not alarmed'.

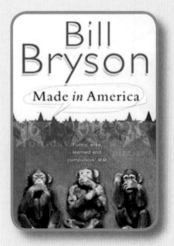

A final feature that contributes to Bryson's lively and engaging style is his use of descriptive language. His choice of **verbs** ('invaded'), **adjectives** ('bewildering') and **nouns** ('<u>obsequiousness</u>') is particularly expressive and adds to the reader's enjoyment of the text.

Using a personal **anecdote**, make **a hook for an article** on the title 'The Power of Advertising in Our Lives'. Use the techniques below as a helping hand and, if you like, read the exemplar for inspiration!

Exemplar: Seeing my name

While out walking recently my attention was drawn to a large poster on the side of a bus. It caught my eye because, in the universally recognised font of white letters on red, it spelled out my name. I was famous. People wanted to share a Coke with me. I was about to seek out the nearest shop to purchase my namesake when a question crossed my mind: how did a syrupy drink invented by a pharmacist in the 1880s become a cultural phenomenon? Because of advertising, of course! I suppose anything can be successful if it's packaged and sold in the right way.

Techniques: Hook using personal anecdote

- In relation to the title, think of an experience you had at a particular time and in a particular place.
- Describe this experience in a clear, <u>concise</u> manner.
- Provide descriptive detail to bring the text to life.
- The questions and reflections the experience stimulated in you will then provide a natural introduction to your article.

READ–ANALYSE–MAKE: Discursive Essay Two

Zadie Smith is a British novelist, essayist and short story writer. The following extract from 'Generation Why?', her review of the 2010 film *The Social Network*, was published in the *New York Review of Books*. The film portrays the founding of Facebook by Mark Zuckerberg.

from 'Generation Why?' by Zadie Smith

I must be in Mark Zuckerberg's generation – there are only nine years between us – but somehow it doesn't feel that way despite the fact that I can say (like everyone else on Harvard's campus in the fall of 2003) that "I was there" at Facebook's inception. At the time I felt distant from Zuckerberg and all the kids at Harvard. I still feel distant from them now, ever more so, as I increasingly opt out (by choice, by default) of the things they have embraced. We have different ideas about things. Specifically we have different ideas about what a person is, or should be.

You want to be optimistic about your own generation. You want to keep pace with them and not to fear what you don't understand. To put it another way, if you feel discomfort at the world they're making, you want to have a good reason for it. Master programmer and virtual reality pioneer Jaron Lanier is not of my generation, but he knows and understands us well, and has written a short and frightening book, *You Are Not a Gadget*, which chimes with my own discomfort, while coming from a position of real knowledge and insight, both practical and philosophical.

Lanier is interested in the ways in which people "reduce themselves" in order to make a computer's description of them appear more accurate. "Information systems," he writes, "need to have information in order to run, but information *underrepresents reality*" (my italics). In Lanier's view, there is no perfect computer analogue for what we call a "person". In life, we all profess to know this, but when we get online it becomes easy to forget. In Facebook, as it is with other online social networks, life is turned into a database, and this is a degradation, Lanier argues, which is "based on a philosophical mistake . . . the belief that computers can presently represent human thought or human relationships. These are things computers cannot currently do."

We know the consequences of this instinctively; we feel them. We know that having two thousand Facebook friends is not what it looks like. We know that we are using the software to behave in a certain, superficial way toward others. We know what we are doing "in" the software. But do we know, are we alert to, what the software is doing to us? Is it possible that what is communicated between people online "eventually becomes their truth"? What Lanier, a software expert, reveals to me, a software idiot, is what must be obvious (to software experts): software is not neutral. Different software embeds different philosophies, and these philosophies, as they become ubiquitous, become invisible.

Lanier asks us to consider, for example, the humble file, or rather, to consider a world without "files". I confess this thought experiment stumped me about as much as if I'd been asked to consider persisting in a world without "time". And then consider further that these designs, so often taken up in a slap-dash, last-minute fashion, become "locked in", and, because they are software, used by millions, too often become impossible to adapt, or change.

Lanier wants us to be attentive to the software into which we are "locked in". Is it really fulfilling our needs? Or are we reducing the needs we feel in order to convince ourselves that the software isn't limited? As Lanier argues: "Different media designs stimulate different potentials in human nature. We shouldn't seek to make the pack mentality as efficient as possible. We should instead seek to inspire the phenomenon of individual intelligence."

But the pack mentality is precisely what Open Graph, a Facebook innovation, is designed to encourage. Open Graph allows you to see everything your friends are reading, watching, eating, so that you might read and watch and eat as they do. "You have to be somebody," Lanier writes, "before you can share yourself." But to Zuckerberg sharing your choices with everybody (and doing what they do) *is* being somebody.

With Facebook, Zuckerberg seems to be trying to create an Internet with one mind, a uniform environment in which it genuinely doesn't matter who you are, as long as you make "choices" (which means, finally, purchases). If the aim is to be liked by more and more people, whatever is unusual about a person gets flattened out. One nation under a format. To ourselves, we are special people, documented in wonderful photos, and it also happens that we sometimes buy things. This latter fact is an incidental matter, to us. However, the advertising money that will rain down on Facebook—if and when Zuckerberg succeeds in encouraging 500 million people to take their Facebook identities onto the Internet at large— this money thinks of us the other way around. To the advertisers, we are our capacity to buy, attached to a few personal, irrelevant photos. Is it possible that we have begun to think of ourselves that way?

ANALYSE

This is an excellent example of a serious discursive text. Smith's **hook** is a personal **anecdote** recounting the fact that she was at Harvard at the same time as Mark Zuckerberg, which is effective in arousing the reader's interest. The subject of the text, 'what a person is, or should be', is also introduced in the first paragraph.

The structural development of the text is logical. Following the hook, each paragraph discusses a particular point relating to the topic. The points discussed are: Smith's discomfort with the world her generation is making, that computers cannot represent human thoughts/relationships, that computer software is not neutral, that software becomes impossible to adapt or change, that software should not be encouraging a pack mentality, and that when human beings become data they are reduced to uniformity.

The text employs a **circular structure**, since the final question posed by Smith – 'Is it possible that we have begun to think of ourselves that way?' – echoes the subject – 'what a person is, or should be' – introduced in the opening paragraph.

The text is written in a style that is forceful and engaging. This is due, to a large extent, to the evidence employed by Smith to illustrate the points made in the text. On a number of occasions she references or quotes directly from Jaron Lanier's book *You Are Not a Gadget*. She also employs **concrete illustration** to support her points: 'Open Graph allows you to see everything'.

Persuasive devices are also used to create a forceful and engaging style. Smith's tone is **subjective** and she employs, at times, an informal **register**: 'I confess this thought experiment stumped me'. This personal and relaxed tone is successful in engaging the reader. The first person plural is often employed (that is, Smith writes 'we' rather than 'I') and this has the effect of involving the reader in her argument. **Rhetorical questions** are used effectively throughout, both to engage the reader's interest with the issues being discussed and to sharpen the presentation of these issues.

Finally, Smith's use of language contributes strongly to her forceful and engaging style. She uses **hyperbole** ('frightening book'), **compound words** ('slap-dash') and **metaphor** ('money that will rain down on Facebook') to strengthen the impact on the reader.

MAKE

Using a description of a scene, make **a hook** **for a speech** on the title 'Technology Affects Young People's Social Interaction'. Use the techniques below as a helping hand and, if you like, read the exemplar for inspiration!

Exemplar: Technology – a dangerous babysitter?

It is a typical television advertisement. A MOTHER is pictured in a large show-house kitchen. CUT to calendar indicating that school summer holidays are approaching. CUT to anxious look on MOTHER's face. CUT to happy family trip to computer store. CUT to three happy children: OLDER BOY on computer in attic bedroom, YOUNG GIRL on dance mat in front of TV with headphones on, YOUNGER BOY sitting on sofa playing Nintendo DS. CUT to MOTHER with cup of tea and contented expression. Advertising presents technology as a great way to keep children and teenagers entertained. But is it? What will these children say to each other, or to their mother, when they gather around the dinner table? LOL? BRB? IDK? Whether we like it or not, technology affects young people's social interaction.

Techniques: Hook using description of a scene

- Select a specific scene that is also universally recognisable.
- Focus on how this scene is representative of a trend or a cultural norm.
- Provide descriptive detail to bring the scene to life.
- The questions and reflections the scene stimulates in you will then provide a natural introduction to your **speech**.

Exam tips for discursive essays

As you will note from the instructions to Leaving Certificate correctors and the extracts from the 2008 Chief Examiner's Report reproduced below, a sense of audience, a clearly established **register**, a logical and coherent structure and the use of persuasive techniques are all highly rewarded in the discursive essay. Conversely, ignoring the intended audience, an inability to focus on the topic, uneven development and the use of **cliché** are all penalised.

Instructions to correctors in the marking schemes of Leaving Certificate 2008–2012 discursive essay compositions

2008

Question 1: '. . . advised adults to treat adolescents with sympathy, appreciation and respect . . .' Write a magazine article (serious and/or light-hearted) in which you give advice to adults on how to help teenagers cope with the 'storm and stress' of adolescence.

Instruction to correctors: Reward a clearly established register and sense of audience appropriate to a magazine. The advice should be rooted in the context of adolescence, but may range widely (personal, practical, etc.).

Chief Examiner's remarks: This popular choice allowed many candidates to take an informative and/or discursive approach. Less successful attempts focused on adolescence in general without any clear sense of direction or audience. While there were many amusing and well-written pieces, some lapsed into cliché.

Question 2: '. . . the new global society.' Write a speech in which you argue for or against the necessity to protect national culture and identity.

Instruction to correctors: Expect candidates to deliver a coherent and cogent argument (for or against). Allow for a broad interpretation of 'national culture and identity'. Reward the candidate's attempt to persuade an audience.

Discursive WRITING

Chief Examiner's remarks: Not a popular choice. The most successful attempts presented spirited arguments in support of national culture – particularly the Irish language and Gaelic games. Many used persuasive techniques effectively and had a very good sense of audience. However, a minority focused on the prompt alone and discussed the modern global society in general terms.

Question 5: '. . . fake, or worse . . .' Write the text of a talk you would deliver to your classmates on the topic: *Appearances can be Deceptive.*

Instruction to correctors: Reward clear evidence of appropriate register and awareness of audience. Allow a broad interpretation of the statement: 'Appearances can be Deceptive'. Expect a variety of approaches – discursive, personal, **narrative**, persuasive, **ironic**, etc.

Chief Examiner's remarks: Relatively few candidates chose this. However, some of the more successful attempts combined a clear thematic approach with an appropriate 'talk' register. Shakespeare's Iago proved a useful starting point for a small number of candidates.

2009

Question 1: '. . . a living classroom . . .' Write an article (serious and/or light-hearted) for a school magazine about your experience of education over the last number of years.

Instruction to correctors: Reward a clearly established register and sense of audience appropriate to a school magazine. Allow for a liberal interpretation of 'education'.

2010

Question 5: 'But there is hopeful news as well . . .' You have been elected by your classmates to deliver a speech at your school's graduation ceremony. Write the text of the speech you would give, encouraging your audience to be optimistic about the future.

Instruction to correctors: Reward candidates' sense of school audience/occasion and their attempts to be persuasive/positive about the future.

2011

Question 2: 'I don't discriminate . . .' Write an article for a serious newspaper or magazine on the twin issues of discrimination and tolerance.

Instruction to correctors: Reward a clearly established and sustained register appropriate to a serious newspaper or magazine. Candidates may adopt a variety of approaches – discursive, informative, personal, narrative, etc. – but should refer to both discrimination and tolerance, though not necessarily equally.

2012

Question 5: '. . . all the time in the world . . .' Write a light-hearted and entertaining article, intended for publication in a magazine aimed at young people, in response to the phrase, 'all the time in the world'.

Instruction to correctors: Reward a clearly established and sustained register appropriate to a publication aimed at young people. Candidates may choose to adopt various approaches (discursive, descriptive, humorous, personal narrative, etc.), but expect a light-hearted, entertaining quality to the writing. Allow for a broad interpretation of 'all the time in the world'.

Discursive WRITING

READ–ANALYSE–MAKE

Read the discursive essay below, written by a sixth-year student in response to the task:

'It's just not fair . . .'

Write a speech in which you argue for or against the provision of free third-level education for all students.

Discursive WRITING

READ

Student exemplar: Free third-level education

Ladies and gentlemen,

Ireland stands at a crossroads. In our country, all major political parties wish to remove the provision of free education and free student fees. Fianna Fáil, Fine Gael and the Labour Party have all stated in their electoral manifestos that they support the re-introduction of fees for third-level students. It appears clear that, at present, the conviction of all political parties is that education is a privilege, not a right. They are wrong. We must stand <u>unequivocal</u> in our defence of free education. If this first step in dismantling our education system is sanctioned, abhorrent consequences will permeate through Irish society. I tell you today, my friends, that this will lead to our destruction.

Education is a right. We live in a society that cherishes the rights of its citizens. *Bunreacht na hÉireann* states that the citizens of this island will attempt to live together to promote 'the common good'. This means people enacting stewardship, respect and responsibility. If this first step in dismantling free third-level fees is allowed to take place, a culture will develop – a culture that does not value education, a culture that does not respect education as a right, a culture that will lead to a weaker society. We need free education so as to uphold these qualities that we in Ireland cherish today.

But the provision of free education also has the utmost economic value for Ireland. Our country does not possess any substantial natural resources to export. We must create a workforce that is well educated and highly skilled. Is it not our primary economic purpose to promote foreign direct investment? The American Chamber of Commerce Ireland has recently stated that it is Ireland's flexible, talented and educated workforce which promotes our country as an attractive region to invest in. Free education for all will allow this to continue. It has been estimated that since third-level fees were funded by the state, over 80,000 extra people annually have entered into education. It is this fact that allowed Ireland to develop and prosper. If we withhold this right from our citizens we will be effectively committing economic suicide.

Yet education provides so much more than economic development. If we withdraw the provision of free education to third-level students, we will widen the class divide so prevalent in today's society. Children who come from disadvantaged backgrounds are three times less likely to enter higher education. Adding yet another barrier to accessing third-level education will reinforce this class division. This has been the case with our European colleagues in Denmark, where the election of a centre-right government in early 2006 saw the reinstatement of third-level fees. And, unsurprisingly, this led to the participation rate in higher education falling by 8 per cent in little under a year. I ask you, ladies and gentlemen, do you really want this to occur here?

But I must emphasise that free third-level education is not only important in relation to economic and demographic concerns. Through free education, our society has been enriched. Society can change for the better. In 2010 the Irish people voted John Hume as the greatest Irish person. Hume grew up in Derry during a time of great injustice against Catholics in the city. He could quite easily have followed the example set by some of his fellow nationalists and taken part in the atrocities of the Troubles. But Hume did not. He helped establish the SDLP and that political party assisted in finding a peaceful solution to the North's problems. And why did Hume 'turn the other cheek'? Because of free education. He was one of the first benefactors of the 1947 Education Act in Britain, which allowed him to attend secondary school for free. Ladies and gentlemen, if free education had not been provided to John Hume, he would not have played such a leading role in implementing the Good Friday Agreement. Undoubtedly, free education for all is at the heart of a democratic and peaceful society.

Ladies and gentlemen, we stand at a crossroads today. Let us not take the road that will lead to future generations of children being less educated, less fulfilled and less enthused than their parents. Instead, let us take the road that leads to a fair and just society in which all children have equal opportunity. Let us make third-level education free for all!

Thank you.

ANALYSE

This is an excellent example of a discursive essay. It follows the recommended structure of beginning with a **hook**, in this case an arresting statement: 'Ireland stands at a crossroads.' The topic, 'we must stand unequivocal in defence of free education', is then introduced and developed in the **body** of the essay, which consists of a series of paragraphs, each addressing a particular point. Evidence (facts, statistics and **concrete illustrations**) is used to support each point. The conclusion consists of a brief summary of the main points and demonstrates the use of **circular structure**: 'Ladies and gentlemen, we stand at a crossroads today.'

The student also employs persuasive techniques, such as **rhetorical questions**, **triadic structures** and **contrast**, to great effect, while forceful language adds to the impassioned tone that is essential to an argumentative **speech**.

Discursive WRITING

MAKE

Write **a discursive essay** about your hopes and fears for the future using the following structure as a helping hand:

> Opening (1 paragraph): begin your essay with a **hook** and introduce the topic.

> Development (3–7 paragraphs): each paragraph must contain a point supported by evidence; keep your writing lively by using descriptive detail and persuasive techniques.

> Conclusion (1 paragraph): end your essay by briefly summarising your main points and employing a **circular structure**, linking back to the hook.

Over to you: Make

Write a discursive essay on any of the following:

1 '. . . such creative manipulation still goes on.' (*Made in America*)

   Write the text of the address you would deliver to an international audience of young people on the dangers of being easily manipulated.

2 'You want to be optimistic about your own generation.' ('Generation Why?')

   Write an article intended for publication in a magazine for young people in which you discuss what there is to be optimistic about in your own generation.

3 '. . . let us take the road that leads to a fair and just society . . .' ('It's just not fair')

   Write an article intended for publication in a serious magazine or newspaper in which you argue for or against the view that 'A fair and just society will never exist'.

4 '. . . a uniform environment in which it genuinely doesn't matter who you are . . .' ('Generation Why?')

   Write the text of a speech to be delivered to an adult audience about what can be done to protect and promote individuality.

5 '. . . and other grammatical manglings . . .' (*Made in America*)

   Write a newspaper or magazine feature article entitled 'Does it matter how we say it when everyone knows what we mean?'

> **Remember**
>
> Leaving Certificate compositions should be between 750 and 1,000 words. You have ten minutes to plan your composition and one hour to write it. The most important criteria for achieving a good grade are that you write consistently on the title you have chosen and that you use a **register** that suits the **genre** of the title. After that, marks are awarded for good structure and paragraphing, clear and fluent expression and correct grammar and spelling.

Discursive WRITING

Narrative

WRITING

 Travel writing

 Fiction

 Novel and modern fairy tale

 Short story

Travel writing

Introduction

In this unit you will be introduced to **travel writing**, a **genre** that has as its focus accounts of real or imaginary places. It encompasses a number of styles that range from the documentary to the <u>evocative</u>, from the literary to the journalistic and from the humorous to the serious. Effective travel writing offers the reader a vivid recollection of the area(s) being described in a way that is useful and entertaining. Travel writing of various degrees of quality may be found on websites, in magazines and in books. A travelogue is a text-film or photographic journal/essay about the places visited and experiences encountered by a traveller. Literary travelogues generally exhibit **narrative** and descriptive qualities beyond the information found in travel journals. In recent years travel **blogs**, known as 'travelogs', have become increasingly popular.

One of the world's leading travel writers, Jan Morris, has said that 'the best travel writers are not really writing about travel at all. They are recording the effects of places or movements on their own particular temperaments – recording the experience rather than the event.' It is not, therefore, the places being written about that are the most important factor, but how the travel writers observe and report what they see.

READ–ANALYSE–MAKE

Joseph Roth, an Austrian-Jewish writer, was the most renowned correspondent in Weimar Germany and produced a series of short essays that influenced a generation of writers. The following extract is from *What I Saw*, which was published in 1921, and is translated by Michael Hoffman.

from *What I Saw* by Joseph Roth

What I see, what I see. What I see is the day in all its absurdity and triviality. A horse, harnessed to a cab, staring with lowered head into its nose bag, not knowing that horses originally came into the world without cabs: a small boy playing with marbles on the sidewalk. He watches the purposeful bustle of the grownups all around him, and, himself full of the delights of idleness has no inkling that he already represents the acme of creation, but instead yearns to be grown up; a policeman who fancies himself as the still point at the centre of a whirlpool of activity, and the pillar of authority – enemy to the street, and placed there to supervise it and accept its tribute in the form of good order.

I see a girl, framed in an open window, who is part of the wall and yearns to be freed from its embrace, which is all she knows of the world. A man, pressed into the shadows of a public square, collecting bits of paper and cigarette butts. An advertising kiosk placed at the head of a street, like its epigram, with a little weathervane on it to proclaim which way the wind is blowing down that particular street. A fat man in a cream-coloured jacket, smoking a cigar, he looks like a grease spot in human form on this summer's day. A café terrace planted with colourful ladies, waiting to be plucked. White-jacketed waiters, navy blue porters, newspaper sellers, a hotel, an elevator boy, a Negro*.

What I see is the old man with the tin trumpet on the Kurfurstendamm. He is a beggar whose plight draws all the more attention to itself for being inaudible. Sometimes the falsetto of the little tin trumpet is stronger and more powerful than the entire Kurfurstendamm. And the motion of a waiter on the café terrace, swishing at a fly, has more content in it than the lives of all the customers on the café terrace. The fly gets away, and the waiter is disappointed. Why so much hostility to a fly, O waiter?

Berlin's Potsdamer Platz as seen from Café Josty (c. 1930)

Narrative WRITING

A war cripple* who finds a nail file. Someone, a lady, has lost the nail file in the place where he happens to sit down. Of course the beggar starts filing his nails – what else is he to do? The coincidence that has left the nail file in his possession and the trifling movement of filing his nails are enough to lift him about a thousand social classes, symbolically speaking. A dog running after a ball, then stopping in front of it, static now and inanimate – unable to grasp how some stupid, brainless rubber thing only a moment ago could have been so lively and spirited – is the hero of a momentary drama. It's only the <u>minutiae</u> of life that are important.

Strolling around on a May morning, what do I care about the vast issues of world history as expressed in newspaper editorials? Or even the fate of some individual, a potential tragic hero, someone who has lost his wife or come into an inheritance or cheated on his wife or in one way or another makes some lofty appeal to us? Confronted with the truly microscopic, all loftiness is hopeless, completely meaningless. The <u>diminutive</u> of the parts is more impressive than the monumentality of the whole. I no longer have any use for the sweeping gestures of heroes on the global stage. I'm going for a walk.

Note on language use

The words marked * in the above extract are now considered outdated and offensive. They were not, however, outdated or offensive at the time Joseph Roth wrote the text.

The way we use language is not static. It changes to reflect the values and attitudes of the society we live in. There is an ongoing **debate** in education about language that is considered outdated and offensive. One side believes that texts should be 'cleansed' of such language to make them comply with current standards; for example, in many schools and universities in the United States the N-word has been removed from Mark Twain's classic novel *Huckleberry Finn*. The other side of the argument is that facing the truth of history and talking about it is a better strategy. What do you think?

Narrative WRITING

ANALYSE

Written text

This is an observational piece. *What* Joseph Roth describes (scenes of city life) is ordinary, but *how* he describes it is extraordinary. This is the mark of a great writer: the ability to make the reader look at life in a new way. At the outset Roth repeats the key phrase 'what I see' in order to emphasise his intention to look closely at ordinary life in all its absurdity and triviality. If something is absurd it is unreasonable and illogical, while something trivial is of little value. This is Roth's theme, that ordinary life is ridiculous and insignificant, and yet, as he concludes in the penultimate paragraph, 'It's only the <u>minutiae</u> of life that are important.'

Following the introductory sentences, Roth develops his theme. In the first paragraph he demonstrates the absurdity of a horse that does not know 'that horses originally came into the world without cabs'; of a boy who 'has no inkling that he already represents the <u>acme</u> of creation' and wants to be a grown-up; and of a policeman who doesn't know that he is an 'enemy to the street'.

In the next paragraph Roth continues to describe what he sees: a girl, a man, an advertising kiosk, a fat man and a group of women. A striking **simile** is used to capture the appearance of the fat man: 'he looks like a grease spot in human form on this summer's day'. A **metaphor** is effectively employed to create a unique image of the group of women: 'A café terrace planted with colourful ladies, waiting to be plucked.' Roth completes this paragraph with a list of observations that add detail and a lively rhythm to the text.

Roth begins the third paragraph by restating the phrase 'what I see', which focuses the reader's attention once more on the theme of the text. Roth's observations here include a beggar, a waiter, a war veteran and a dog. Each description highlights the random and crazy nature of existence: the waiter is obsessed with a fly, while the war veteran files his nails. Roth is accumulating evidence so that when he gets to the point of his text – 'It's only the <u>minutiae</u> of life that are important' – the reader is already convinced.

In the final paragraph Roth expands on this central point. He employs two consecutive **rhetorical questions** to add energy and urgency to his argument and concludes with a definitive statement: 'The <u>diminutive</u> of the parts is more impressive than the monumentality of the whole.' It is ordinary life that interests Roth and he is, therefore, as the last sentence tells us, 'going for a walk'.

Visual text

The **visual** text accompanying the extract from *What I Saw* depicts a city scene from Berlin in the 1920s. There is too much detail in the black-and-white photograph for it to be used in the Leaving Certificate exam paper, but it is included here, not only because it complements Roth's piece, both in content and atmosphere, but also because of its relevance to one of the hottest topics in the visual arts today: black and white – a new trend?

According to *Variety* magazine, more black-and-white films were released in 2012 and 2013 than during any other comparable time frame in recent history. Directors are choosing the medium for a variety of reasons, but the general consensus is that black-and-white films (and photos) are suggestive of the following qualities: modesty, <u>austerity</u>, <u>nostalgia</u>, classic style and old Hollywood glamour.

For critic and film-maker Mark Cousins, the format connects us with the most exalted days of the movies. 'Cinema became an art in black and white,' he says, 'and to shoot in black and white still feels, for many film-makers, like being among the gods.'

Poster for 2012 Spanish black-and-white silent fantasy film *Blancanieves*

Narrative WRITING

MAKE

QUESTION B

Draft the text of **a feature advertisement** to be published in the travel section of a newspaper. The copy should entice readers to visit a particular city. Name the city and offer a descriptive account of its attractions. (50)

Sample answer

Summer in Dublin

Summer is the perfect time to visit the city of Dublin. The events of James Joyce's novel *Ulysses* take place on a summer's day, 16 June 1904, in Dublin, and every year on the anniversary of the date the city celebrates 'Bloomsday'. But whether your tastes are literary or not, you will always, as the lyrics go, 'remember that summer in Dublin'.

Start your day with breakfast in one of the city's many cafés. In recent years Dublin has embraced the café culture of Europe and you can sit in the early-morning sun sipping a latte while the world goes by around you – young professionals walking to work in suits and running shoes, older residents perambulating in a more leisurely fashion, children and young people gathering together to travel to the various beaches or parks that are situated in such close proximity to the city.

After breakfast take a stroll down Grafton Street, the main shopping boulevard, and then around the more <u>eclectic</u> quarter of the city known as Temple Bar. Whatever your tastes or budget, Dublin caters for it. You can browse among the moneyed classes in a world-renowned department store and afterwards pick up an old vinyl record in a poky little second-hand shop. Dublin is full of side streets and hidden gems. Take your time and wander freely in this miniature metropolis.

During the years of economic boom the city of Dublin benefited from the arrival of immigrants who brought with them their culture and cuisine, resulting in the <u>cosmopolitan</u> lifestyle in evidence today. Gone is the somewhat grey and insular city of older times. Dublin is now awash with vibrant colour and bustling with city life. You can have lunch in a Lebanese, Thai or Polish restaurant and soak up the atmosphere of a city that is retaining its traditions while embracing new influences. And this exciting mixture of the old and the new is everywhere. After lunch you can take in the glories of Christ Church, the oldest cathedral in Dublin, and also visit the glass and steel architecture of Dublin's Docklands, the most ambitious urban regeneration project in Ireland's history.

By night Dublin city really comes alive. On bright summer evenings city workers leave the office behind them and take their seats on the terraces of trendy wine bars while older residents enjoy the entertainments the city has to offer – theatre, music concerts and international sporting events – and young people, tired after a day on the beach, sit around in parks, like colourful confetti scattered over the green lawns.

Narrative WRITING

Techniques: Advertisement

- Advertising has a dual function. It must inform consumers of the product while also persuading them to make a particular choice.
- Layout is important. Give your advertisement a heading and a subheading. Write the **copy** in a series of short paragraphs. You may give instructions for the inclusion of a **visual**.
- Advertising copy typically employs <u>superlatives</u>, **hyperbole** and <u>buzzwords</u>.
- Advertisements are aimed at particular groups within society. Employ a **register** that is appropriate to the target audience of your advertisement (gender, age, socio-economic group).

Over to you: Read and analyse

As you read the following text from the 2012 Leaving Certificate exam paper, take note of the annotations in the margins and see if you can isolate the particular words and phrases that the annotations refer to. In this way you will improve your skills in both reading and analysing.

Text 3, 2012: A journey remembered and revisited

This text is adapted from Paul Theroux's book entitled *Ghost Train to the Eastern Star*. In this edited extract he describes travelling like a 'ghost' through his own memories as he revisits places he had experienced earlier in his life.

Longer sentences create a reflective mood

Effective use of simile

Use of second person involves reader in the text

Observations on memory and the past create a thoughtful text

Adjectives and auditory imagery bring memories to life

Travel can induce such a distinct and nameless feeling of strangeness and disconnection in me that I feel insubstantial, like a puff of smoke, merely a ghost, a creepy <u>spectre</u> from the underworld, unobserved and watchful among real people, wandering, listening while remaining unseen. Being invisible – the usual condition of the older traveller – is much more useful than being obvious. Ghosts have all the time in the world, another pleasure of long-distance aimlessness. And this ghostliness, I was to find, was also an effect of the journey I had chosen, returning to places I had known many years ago. It is almost impossible to return to an early scene in your travelling life and not feel like a spectre. And many places I saw were themselves sad and spectral, while I was the haunting presence, the eavesdropping shadow on the ghost train.

Long after I took the trip I wrote about in *The Great Railway Bazaar*, I went on thinking how I'd gone overland, changing trains across Asia, improvising my trip, rubbing against the world. And reflecting on what I'd seen – the way the unrevisited past is always looping in your dreams. Memory is a ghost train too. Ages later you still ponder the beautiful face you once glimpsed in a distant country; the sight of a noble tree, or a country road, or a happy tale in a café, or the sound of a train at night, striking that precise musical note of train whistles.

*Extended ghost **metaphor** creates memorable images*

*Unusual **verb** evokes robust engagement with the world*

*Extended ghost **metaphor** serves as linking device through the text*

Narrative WRITING

Thirty-three years went by. I was then twice as old as the person who had ridden those trains, most of them pulled by steam locomotives, boiling across the hinterland of Turkey and India. Had my long-ago itinerary changed as much as me? I had the idea of taking the same trip again, travelling in my own footsteps.

Factual information provides context

*Effective use of **rhetorical question***

Assertive statement engages reader's interest

***Juxtaposition** of ideas is provocative*

Details – who, where, what – provide clarity

The decision to return to any early scene in your life is dangerous but irresistible. A great satisfaction in growing old – one of many – is assuming the role of a witness to the wobbling of the world and seeing irreversible changes. Older people are perceived as cynics – but no, they are simply people who have at last heard the still, sad music of humanity played by an inferior rock band howling for fame. Going back and retracing my footsteps would be for me a way of seeing who I was, where I went, and what subsequently happened to the places I had seen.

'The still, sad music of humanity' is a phrase from William Wordsworth's poem 'Tintern Abbey'

Image A

Colour illustration of the front of a train on a track with further black-and-white illustrations in the background

The head-on perspective of the train, with a glimpse of its carriages in the distance, suggests the movement and excitement of a journey

A rough map of Asia suggests adventure and the unknown while the faint sketch of people and train stations conveys a sense of the <u>transitory</u> nature of travel

*Effective use of **adjective** and **noun** to convey point*

The thing to avoid would be the tedious reminiscences of better days, the twittering of the <u>nostalgia</u> bore, whose message is usually *I was there and you weren't*. 'I remember when you could get four of those for a dollar.' 'There was a big tree in a field where that building is now.' 'In my day . . .'

Oh, shut up!

Quotations provide concrete illustration of point

Repeated questions engage reader

What traveller backtracked to take the great trip again? You could ask, 'why should they bother?' Certain poets, notably Wordsworth and Yeats, enlarged their vision and found enlightenment in returning to an earlier landscape of their lives. My proposed trip to retrace the itinerary of *The Great Railway Bazaar* was mainly curiosity on my part, with a hankering to be away.

Reference to poets adds depth to the text

At Waterloo Station I found the right platform for the Eurostar, the 12.09 to Paris. The reminders of my old London were almost immediate. The indifference of Londoners, their brisk way of walking, their fixed expressions, no one wearing a hat in the rain yet some carrying brollies – all of us striding past a gaunt young woman swaddled in dirty quilts, sitting on the wet floor at the foot of some metal steps at the railway station, begging.

Strong visual impressions of London

Information provides specific context

Adjectives sharpen the detailed description

I was a few minutes out of Waterloo, clattering across the shiny rain-drenched rails of Clapham Junction, thinking: I have been here before. On the line through south London, my haunted face at the window, my former life as a Londoner began to pass before my eyes. I got a glimpse of a cinema I had gone to until it became a bingo hall, the church that was turned into a daycare centre. Beyond the common the Alfarthing Primary School, where my kids, all pale faces and skinny legs, were taught to sing by Mrs Quarmby. These were streets I knew well: one where my bike was stolen, another where my car was broken into; greengrocers and butcher shops where I'd shopped; the chippie, the florist, the Chinese grocer, the newsagent, an Indian from Mwanza who liked speaking Swahili with me because he missed the shores of Lake Victoria. From scenes like these I had made my London life.

Extended ghost metaphor serves as a linking device

Inclusion of proper names adds to realism of the text

Onomatopoeic verb offers a startling auditory image

Concrete illustrations illustrate theme of change

Personal tone throughout creates an intimate relationship between writer and reader

But the wonderful thing was that I was whisked through south London with such efficiency, I was spared the deeper pain of looking closely at the past. I was snaking through tunnels and across viaducts and railway cuttings, looking left and right at the landscape of my personal history and, happily, moving on, to other places that held no ambiguous memories.

Verbs create a sense of fluid movement

Image B

Black-and-white photograph of train moving through a station. The most striking effect in the visual is the blurring of the train. Its streaked lights capture the fact that the train is moving at speed, suggesting the rapid passage of time and of life itself

The static, solid and clearly defined station contrasts powerfully with the speeding, ghostly and vague blur of the passing train. The platforms are empty and this, with the absence of colour, creates a downbeat, somewhat melancholy atmosphere, suggestive of night-time

Narrative WRITING

113

Answer the following Leaving Certificate questions using the guidelines below.

QUESTION A

 (i) Based on your reading of the above text, what impression do you form of the writer, Paul Theroux? Support your view with reference to the text. (15)

 (ii) Which one of the visual images (**A** or **B**) do you think best illustrates the above text? In your response refer to both visual images. (15)

(iii) Paul Theroux is a successful travel writer. Based on the above passage, what do you think makes his writing attractive to so many readers? In your answer, you should refer to both the content and style of the text. (20)

Answer guidelines

Part (i): begin by explicitly answering the question; for instance, *Based on my reading of the text, I form a strong impression of the writer Paul Theroux.* Focus clearly on one or more aspects of the writer's character/personality. Possible points include: nostalgic, reflective, philosophical nature; whimsical, with a self-deprecating sense of humour; adventurous and observant traveller; sensitive, with a social conscience.

Part (ii): remember, questions on the **visual** text require an analysis of both content and style. Begin by explicitly answering the question; for instance, *I think that visual image B best illustrates this text.* You can nominate either A or B as being the better image to illustrate the text but in justifying your choice you should refer to *both* visual images. Possible points include:

- Image A: composite image (map, train and so on) reflects the writer's journeys; **symbolic impact** of, for example, the colour red, star, track; cartoon quality enhances/diminishes the impact of the text.
- Image B: evocative image reflects the idea of movement and transience; black-and-white image suggests a timeless atmosphere; photograph reinforces/reduces the rich content of the passage.

Part (iii): begin by answering the question; for instance, *Based on my reading of the passage, there are many reasons that make Paul Theroux's writing attractive to so many readers.* While you are free to agree and/or disagree with the question, you must discuss and offer illustrations of one or more aspects of Theroux's writing, referring to both content and style. Possible points include: convincing sense of place, atmosphere and cultural change; perceptive, **narrative** approach is appealing; intimacy of the writer's reflections engages the reader; attractive whimsical humour; evocative, descriptive language is informative and entertaining; effective use of **contrast**.

Over to you: Make

Answer the following Leaving Certificate question using the tips and techniques below.

QUESTION B

Your school's Student Council is currently discussing the issue of school outings, educational trips, theatre visits, etc. Write **a persuasive article for your school website** supporting **or** opposing such events. (50)

Answer tips

You may choose from a broad range of approaches (formal or informal, serious or humorous) to writing the website article, but there should be a persuasive quality to your writing in favour or against such school events. Address all aspects of the task. Take care to demonstrate:

- Clear appreciation of the task
- Consistency of **register**
- Effective reference/illustration
- Quality of your writing.

Techniques: Persuasive website article

- Layout is an important feature of Question B tasks. Organise your answer in imitation of the general layout of a website article: headline, subheading(s), **by-line**, links, side-bar.
- As the **register** of a website article tends to be less formal than that of print articles, employ a relaxed, conversational tone.
- Include evidence to support the points you make. This can be a mixture of soft evidence (**anecdotes** and examples) to illustrate the point and hard evidence (facts, statistics and quotes) to substantiate the point.
- Use persuasive techniques, such as **rhetorical questions**, forceful language, **contrast**, **triadic structures**, **exhortation**, **hyperbole**, to convince the reader of the validity of your case.
- Remember, in all journalistic texts the essential quality is clarity of expression.

Test yourself

In this age of mobile phones, cybercafés and satellite links, it is harder than ever to truly escape . . . but not impossible. Travel writer Dervla Murphy, who has ventured to the ends of the earth with only the most basic provisions, explains how. This text is adapted from an article in the *Guardian* in 2009.

Narrative WRITING

115

from 'First, Buy Your Pack Animal' by Dervla Murphy

The individual traveller's "age of adventure" has long since been ended by "S&T" (science and technology). Now our planet's few remaining undeveloped expanses are accessible only to well-funded expeditions. Happily, it's still possible for individuals to embark on solo journeys through little-known regions where they can imagine how real explorers used to feel.

Image A

Reviewers tend to describe my most exhilarating journeys as "adventures", though to me they are a form of escapism – a concept unfairly tainted with negative connotations. If journeys are designed as alternatives to one's everyday routine, why shouldn't they be escapist? To facilitate escapism, I offer the following tips . . .

1. **Choose your country, use guidebooks to identify the areas most frequented by foreigners – and then go in the opposite direction.**

   The escapist traveller needs space, solitude, silence. Tragically, during my lifetime, roads have drastically depleted that natural habitat. Adverts for phoney "adventure tours" make me grind my few remaining teeth. For example, "England to Kenya by truck! Overland adventure! See five countries in six weeks!" Who in their right mind wants to see five countries in six weeks? I always try to get off the beaten track.

2. **Mug up on history.**

   To travel in ignorance of a region's history leaves you unable to understand the "why" of anything or anyone. Learn as much as possible about religious and social taboos, and then scrupulously respect them.

3. **Travel alone, or with just one prepubescent child.**

   In some countries even two adults may be perceived as providing mutual support, making acceptability by the locals less spontaneous and complete. Au contraire, a child's presence emphasises your trust in the community's goodwill. And because children pay little attention to racial or cultural differences, junior companions rapidly demolish barriers of shyness or apprehension often raised when foreigners unexpectedly approach a remote village.

4. **Don't overplan.**

   At sunrise it's not necessary – nor even desirable – to know where you are going to be at sunset. In sparsely inhabited areas carry a lightweight tent and sleeping bag. Elsewhere, rely on fate to provide shelter: dependence on those met en route greatly enhances escapism, and villagers are unfailingly hospitable to those who trust them.

5. **Be self-propelling: walk or cycle.**

   For long treks, far from roads and towns, buy a pack animal to carry food, camping gear, kerosene for your stove if firewood is scarce. It's important to travel light. At least 75% of the equipment sold nowadays in camping shops – travel clotheslines, rolled-up camping mats, lightweight hairdryers – is superfluous. My primary basics, although it depends on the journey, are a lightweight tent, a sleeping bag suitable for the country's temperature, and a stove.

Image B

Narrative WRITING

6. **Cyberspace intercourse <u>vitiates</u> genuine escapism.**

Abandon your mobile phone, laptop, i-Pod and all such links to family, friends and work colleagues. Concentrate on where you are, deriving your entertainment from immediate stimuli, the tangible world around you. Increasingly, in hostels and guesthouses, one sees "independent" travellers eagerly settling down in front of computers instead of conversing with fellow travellers. They seem only partially "abroad", unable to cut their links with home. Evidently the nanny state – and the trend among parents to over-protect offspring – has alarmingly diminished the younger generation's self-reliance. And who is to blame for this entrapment in cyberspace? Who but the fussy folk back at base, awaiting the daily (even twice daily) email of reassurance.

7. **Don't be inhibited by the language barrier.**

Our basic needs – sleeping, eating, drinking – can always be indicated by signs or globally understood noises. Even on the emotional level, the language barrier is quite porous. People's features – particularly their eyes – are wonderfully <u>eloquent</u>.

8. **Be cautious – cautious as distinct from timid.**

The assumption that only brave or reckless people undertake solo journeys off the beaten track is without foundation. In fact, escapists are ultra cautious: that's one of their hallmarks, and an essential component of their survival mechanisms. Before departure, they suss out likely dangers and either change their route – should these seem excessive – or prepare to deal with any reasonable hazards.

QUESTION A

(i) Escapism, as Dervla Murphy remarks, has a bad reputation. Based on your reading of the above text, what is Murphy's own understanding of 'escapism'? Support your view with reference to the text. (15)

(ii) In your opinion, which one of the two visual portraits, **A** or **B**, of Dervla Murphy accompanying the written text best represents the personality of the author of this article? In your response refer to both visual images. (15)

(iii) 'Good travel writing should be both useful and entertaining.' Do you consider the above extract to be an example of 'good travel writing'? In your response you should refer to both the content and the style of the text. (20)

QUESTION B

'To travel in ignorance of a region's history . . .'

Draft the text of **a feature advertisement** to be published in the travel section of a newspaper, in which you describe the historical **or** cultural **or** natural attractions of a particular region outside Ireland. (50)

Fiction

Introduction

In this unit you will be introduced to **fiction writing**. All **narratives** that are not factual, but rather are imaginary, are known as fiction.

Elements of fiction

- Character: works of fiction usually have main characters and secondary characters. **Characterisation** refers to how the characters are made. They should be realistic and credible and operate from a motivation that has some basis in the plot. The secret to good characterisation is show, don't tell. In other words, show the body language, facial expressions, action, speech and appearance of your character, but don't devote time to telling the reader about the character. Go for depth and detail in your descriptions.

- Plot is not just what happens in a story, but how what happens is managed. Plot is controlled by the structure and time frame of the story. It can be very simple or very complex. Narratives may be **forward moving** or employ **flashback**. They may be chronological or episodic. They may have extremely short time frames or take place over generations.

- Setting refers to the world that the story takes place in. It needs to feel three-dimensional in order for the story to be realistic. Setting is created through the use of the senses and concrete detail.

- Narrative voice refers to who is telling the story. A narrative may be told from a first person, second person, third person or omniscient **point of view**. The choice of narrative voice profoundly affects the way the story is communicated to the reader.

- **Dialogue** is a vital aspect of narrative writing and must be correctly formatted. When using dialogue, follow these three easy rules:

  1 New speaker, new line.

  2 Each piece of dialogue begins with a capital letter.

  3 Place your dialogue within speech marks and use a comma between dialogue and tag; for example, 'Hi,' said Sheila. 'How are you?'

- Description: the quality of the writing is what makes a story good. A story should employ **imagery**, **symbols**, carefully chosen **verbs** and **adjectives**, a variety of sentence and paragraph lengths and a rich vocabulary.

- Atmosphere is created through recurring symbols (including colour, light, dark and other evocative elements) and **pathetic fallacy**.

READ–ANALYSE–MAKE

The Waves is an experimental novel published by Virginia Woolf in 1931. It explores the lives and interactions of seven friends. The following extract is an **interior monologue** by one of the characters, Bernard.

from *The Waves* by Virginia Woolf

Heaven be praised for solitude. Let me be alone. Let me cast and throw away this veil of being, this cloud that changes with the least breath, night and day, and all night and all day. While I sat here I have been changing. I have watched the sky change. I have seen clouds cover the stars, then free the stars, then cover the stars again. Now I look at their changing no more. Now no one sees me and I change no more. Heaven be praised for solitude that has removed the pressure of the eye, the solicitation of the body, and all need of lies and phrases.

My book, stuffed with phrases, has dropped to the floor. It lies under the table, to be swept up by the charwoman when she comes wearily at dawn looking for scraps of paper, old tram tickets, and here and there a note screwed into a ball and left with the litter to be swept up. What is the phrase for the moon? And the phrase for love? By what name are we to call death? I do not know. I need a little language such as lovers use, words of one syllable such as children speak when they come into the room and find their mother sewing and pick up some scrap of bright wool, a feather or a shred of chintz. I need a howl; a cry. When the storm crosses the marsh and sweeps over me where I lie in the ditch unregarded I need no words. Nothing neat. Nothing that comes down with all its feet on the floor. None of those resonances and lovely echoes that break and chime from nerve to nerve in our breasts, making wild music, false phrases. I have done with phrases.

How much better is silence; the coffee-cup, the table. How much better to sit by myself like the solitary sea-bird that opens its wings on the stake. Let me sit here for ever with bare things, this coffee-cup, this knife, this fork, things in themselves, myself being myself. Do not come and worry me with your hints that it is time to shut up the shop and be gone. I would willingly give all my money that you should not disturb me but let me sit on and on, silent, alone.

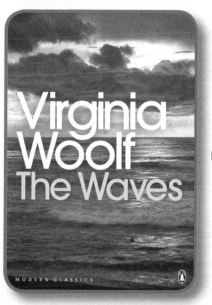
Image 1

Image 2

ANALYSE

Written text

In theatre a **monologue** is a **speech** given by a character on stage to express his or her thoughts aloud. When such a speech is heard only by the audience (and not by any other character in the play), it is known as a soliloquy. In a novel, however, when a character's thoughts are revealed it is known as **interior monologue**. In this extract the thoughts of a character called Bernard on the subject of solitude are revealed.

Virginia Woolf was part of a literary movement known as **modernism** and her work does not adhere to the rules of conventional **narrative**, but instead attempts to capture the rhythm and random nature of the human thought process. The rhythm of the first paragraph is erratic and energetic, mirroring Bernard's mood as he wishes to be alone. He reflects on change, starting with a sudden awareness of the changing nature of his own identity, then noticing the changes in the world about him, and finally pondering on the need to repress his own nature in social interaction with others.

The text is written in a style known as **stream of consciousness**. It reveals Bernard's thoughts as fleeting and disconnected, but all the more real for that. The text is a meditation on the nature of language and how words can be inadequate to express all that exists in the human mind. Bernard is aware of the potential for falsity in language (in books and in phrases) and he seeks a simpler form of expression.

In the third paragraph Bernard has settled on silence as the state he wishes to dwell in. The word 'silence' is used at the beginning of the paragraph and the word 'silent' is used at the end. The intervening images are of simplicity (coffee-cup, table, knife, fork). A **simile** is used by Bernard as a **visual** image of his inner desire 'to sit by myself like the solitary sea-bird'.

Visual text

In the Leaving Certificate examination students are often asked to compare and contrast visual images. Read carefully the following response to the question: Which of the above book covers for *The Waves* do you find more interesting? Note the analysis of both content and style, as well as an exploration of the key differences between landscape and portrait images.

Both covers express a sense of solitude, but Image 1 is more powerful. It effectively uses landscape to create a brooding, desolate mood. It is night-time, with all the unease and uncertainties that that brings. The dark storm clouds in the sky, heavy and black with rain and obscuring the light of the moon, suggest turbulence and gloom. The sea also is unsettled, with heaving and breaking waves reflecting the novel's title. It seems cold, grey, forbidding. The channel of light taken from the invisible moon is not strong enough to either illuminate or warm the surface. The horizon, sharply defined by this light, seems distant, unattainable, but also inviting and challenging.

In contrast, the cover in Image 2 is softer and warmer, offering a much more melancholic and wistful sense of solitude, but not the same complexity. The colours are faint and rather washed out, reflecting the listlessness of the young woman, but sunlight falls on two areas of lush green vegetation, suggesting the possibility of new growth, of life. The swirling, tangled black daubs

Narrative WRITING

behind the figure are troubled and moody, but not as powerfully expressive, or as fluid, as the black clouds on the first cover.

The woman's facial expression is <u>pensive</u>, and somewhat saddened, her head inclines thoughtfully, and she hugs herself consolingly, but the overall effect of her body language is to convey a sense of bitter-sweetness, a much more sentimental tone than the raw energy and extremity of Image 1.

Contemplating Image 2, the viewer becomes an onlooker, an unseen spectator catching a young woman in a moment of private <u>melancholy</u>. With Image 1, one views the landscape, and so becomes a part of that landscape, responding to its contours and colours. Image 1 is, therefore, superior in terms of its <u>impact</u> on the viewer.

Finally, the lettering used on the two covers is markedly different in style and impact. Image 1 uses a large, bold font, with clean, simple lines, against the clear white of the sky for the author's name and steely grey of the sea for the title, all contributing to the elemental power of the image. Probably the most noticeable thing about Image 2's lettering is the pretty intertwining of the two letter Os and the ornamentation of the N, W and A in the author's name. This, I think, encapsulates the differences between the two book covers: the inferior Image 2 is pretty, and ornamental, and a little sentimental; the superior Image 1 is forceful and uncompromising.

QUESTION B

'Heaven be praised for solitude!'

Write **a descriptive passage** on your own experience of solitude. (50)

Sample answer

Hotel room

The door slams shut. I let myself fall against it and feel myself sliding to the floor. The cold wood sucks at the wet skin of my back. I place my contorting hand against my ribs and strain to concentrate on my breaths. Voices still echo around the empty confines of my mind. I close my eyes but I still feel eyes on me. My throat constricts. I reason with myself, 'You're being ridiculous. You're alone now.' And I am. I let my head roll back and concentrate on the slowing of my heartbeat. I inhale. Oxygen reaches my neurons electrifying them into rational thought. I let my shoulders drop.

I crawl over to the bed. The carpet scratches at my knees. The burn is exhilarating. My head hits against the pillow. The fluorescent glare of the alarm clock wakes me at 4.00 a.m. Somewhere outside I hear a cat screaming. 4.05 a.m. With grim resignation I watch a cockroach climb up the bedpost. 4.15 a.m. My neck is stiff. I switch positions. My dress sticks to me, making me itch. I take it off. Light floods the room as a car speeds past. I step over to the moulding curtains and tug them closed. The damp smell begins to choke me. I shove my face into the pillow.

5.15 a.m. I wake to the slamming of an open window next door. My eyes frantically dart around. The cockroach sits on the lampshade with an accusatory glare. My nails scratch against my thigh as I shiver. The breeze unnerves me. I scan the room for movement. There isn't any. My own voice shocks me. I sigh, 'This is ludicrous. I need to get some sleep.' The cockroach twitches. I feel panic rising again so I begin to pace the room. The silence is deafening as my steps become faster. My concentration wanes for an instant and the cold concrete of the wall slaps my cheek. Hot tears salt my tongue as I surrender myself to the cheap polyester carpet.

I jolt into consciousness as light assaults my eyes. A figure, defined by the light of the door, appears. It is the chambermaid. She dismisses my dishevelled appearance with a shrug. I look at the bedside cabinet. There, with all six legs in the air, lies the shrivelled carcass of the cockroach. The chambermaid leaves. I am absolutely alone.

Techniques: Descriptive passage ►►

Among the standard features of good descriptive writing are:

- Creation of credible, engaging characters
- Stimulating use of **metaphor** and **imagery**
- Evocation of atmosphere by means of the weather, seasons, time of day, mood, colour
- Use of **sensory** detail – **visual**, **auditory**, **tactile**, **olfactory** and **gustatory**
- Use of powerful **verbs** to capture action and subtle verbs to capture gesture and movement
- Use of colourful **adjectives** to depict appearance.

Over to you: Read and analyse

As you read the following text from the 2009 Leaving Certificate exam paper, take note of the annotations in the margins and see if you can isolate the particular words and phrases that the annotations refer to. In this way you will improve your skills in both reading and analysing.

Narrative WRITING

Text 2, 2009: Personal decisions

This text is taken from a short story by Australian writer David Malouf entitled 'The Valley of Lagoons'. In this extract, a bookish young teenager longs to join his mates on a hunting trip to the mysterious Valley of Lagoons. The story is set in Brisbane, Australia.

Opening sentences economically introduce the main characters, their relationships, and the hunting motif

Narrative voice is confident and perceptive

Small but significant details give a vivid impression of community

Sense of mystery created through imagery and adjectives

Realistic setting created through precise detail

Landscape precisely captured through its physical features

My father was not a hunting man. When he and my mother first came here in the late nineteen thirties, he'd been invited out, when August came round, on a hunting party to the Lagoons. It was a courtesy, an act of neighbourliness extended to a newcomer, if only to see how he might fit in. "Thanks Gerry," I imagine him saying in his easy way. "Not this time I reckon. Ask me again next year, eh?" And he had said that again the following year, and the year after, until they stopped asking. My father wasn't being stand-offish or condescending. It was simply that hunting, and the grand rigmarole, as he saw it, of gun talk and game talk and dog talk, was not his style.

He had been a soldier in New Guinea and had seen enough perhaps, for one lifetime, of killing. It was an oddness in him that was accepted like any other, humorously, and was perhaps not entirely unexpected in a man who had more books in his house than could be found in the county library.

As the town's only solicitor, he was a respected figure. He was liked. My mother too was an outsider and, despite heavy hints, had not joined the sewing circle and jam-and-chutney-makers. After more than twenty years in the district, my father had never been to the Lagoons, and till I was sixteen I had not been there either, except in the dreamtime of my own imaginings. When I was in third grade at primary school, it was the magic of the name itself that drew me. But it was not marked on the wall-map in our classroom and I could not find it in any atlas, which gave it the status of a secret place. It had a history but only in the telling: in stories I heard from fellows in the playground at school, or from their older brothers at the barbershop.

Just five hours south off a good dirt highway, it was where all the river systems in our quarter of the state have their rising: the big rain-swollen streams that begin in a thousand thread-like runnels and falls in the rainforests, then plunge and gather and flow wide-banked and muddy-watered to the coast. It was the place where the leisurely watercourses make their way inland across plains stacked with anthills and break up and lose themselves in the mudflats and swamps.

Father's mild-mannered character is created through his voice

Colourful, humorous expression reveals something of both the character and the activity

Specific activities define the group as domesticated

Precise references to time provide a realistic context

Graphic imagery brings the scene to life

Vigorous verbs and adjectives enhance the description

Narrative WRITING

Tension and drama created through expectation – the promise of something that might happen

Each year in the first week of August, my friend Braden's father, Wes McGowan, got up a hunting party. I was always invited. My father after a good deal of humming and hawing and using my mother as an excuse, would tell me I was too young and decline to let me go. But I knew he was uneasy about it, and all through the last weeks of July, as talk in the town grew, I waited in the hope he might relent.

Father's uncertainty repeatedly captured through his expressions, both verbal and non-verbal

Time of day, light and weather combine to evoke early morning atmosphere of anticipation

When the day of the hunt came I would get up early, pull on a sweater against the cold and, in the misty half-light just before dawn, jog down the deserted main street, past the last service station at the edge of town, to the river park where the McGowans' truck would be waiting, piled high with tarpaulins, bedrolls, cook-pots, and Braden settled among them with two Labrador retrievers at his feet.

The verb is expressive of the boy's eagerness

Drama heightened by verbs that capture a sense of activity

Old Wes McGowan and Henry Denkler, who was also the town mayor, would be out stretching their legs, stamping their boots on the frosty ground or bending to inspect the tyres. The older McGowan boys, Stuart and Glen, would be squatting on their heels over a smoke. When the second vehicle drew up with Matt Riley and his nephew, Jem, a second inspection would be made of the tyres and the load and then with all the rituals of meeting done, they would climb into the cabin of the truck, and I would be left standing to wave them off; and then jog slowly back home.

Adverb used to capture the boy's mood

The break came in the year after I turned sixteen. When I went for the third or fourth year running to tell my father that the McGowans had offered to take me out to the Lagoons and to ask if I could go, he surprised me by looking up over the top of his glasses and saying, "That's up to you, son. You're old enough, I reckon, to make your own decisions." It was to be Braden's last trip before he went to university. "So," said my father quietly, though he already knew the answer, "what's it to be?" "I'd really like to go," I told him.

"Good," he said, not sounding regretful. "I want you to look out and be careful, that's all. Braden's a sensible enough young fellow. But your mother will worry her soul case out till you're home again." What he meant was, *he* would.

Father's gentleness and affectionate concern are expressed not only in what he says, but also in the tone and rhythms of his speech

Time of day and light evoke atmosphere

Just before sun-up, the McGowans' truck swung uphill to where I was waiting with my duffel bag and bedroll on our front veranda. Behind me, the lights were on in our front room and my mother was there in her dressing gown, with a mug of tea to warm her hands, just inside the screen door. I was glad the others could not see her, and hoped she would not come out at the last moment to kiss me or tuck my scarf into my windcheater. But in fact, "Look after Braden," was all she said as I waved and shouted "See you" over my shoulder and took three leaps down to the front gate.

Contrast between the boy's scarf and his mother's dressing gown encapsulates the separation between them and his growing independence

Final movement of the boy conveys his eagerness

Answer the following Leaving Certificate questions using the guidelines below.

QUESTION A

(i) David Malouf <u>evokes</u> a strong sense of place in this extract from his short story. What impression do you get of the Australian town and its people? Support your answer with reference to the text. (15)

(ii) Do you think the boy has a good relationship with his parents? Give reasons for your answer. (15)

(iii) Identify and comment on **four** features of narrative and/or descriptive writing evident in this text. Support your answer by illustration from the text. (20)

Answer guidelines

Part (i): begin by explicitly answering the question; for instance, *David Malouf evokes a strong sense of place in this extract from his short story. I get a strong impression of the Australian town and its people*. Then discuss one or more features of the town and its people. Possible points include: family/community 'neighbourliness'; traditional social activities; distinctive natural landscape; conservative, isolated atmosphere.

Part (ii): begin by explicitly answering the question; for instance, *I think the boy has a good relationship with his parents*. Then discuss of one or more characteristics of the boy's relationship with both parents (though not necessarily equally). Possible points include: regard for his father: 'a respected figure'; appreciation of his mother: 'an outsider'; passive acceptance of parental authority; <u>intuitive</u> awareness of his parents' close relationship; reserved sensitivity or embarrassment within the family.

Part (iii): begin by answering the question; for instance, *There are many features of narrative and/or descriptive writing evident in this text*. Then discuss and provide illustration of four features of **narrative** and/or descriptive style. Possible points include: <u>evocative</u> setting, atmosphere; effective **characterisation** and **dialogue**; strong narrative voice; detailed, vivid images; striking **verbs** and **adjectives**.

Over to you: Make

Answer the following Leaving Certificate question using the tips and techniques below.

QUESTION B

'You're old enough, I reckon, to make your own decisions.'

Write **a short speech** in which you attempt to persuade a group of parents that older teenagers should be trusted to make their own decisions. (50)

Answer tips

You are free to choose from a broad range of persuasive approaches: personal, informative, humorous, **anecdotal** and so on. You should convey a sustained sense of audience and give a focused treatment of 'should be trusted to make their own decisions'.

Evidence of the following will be rewarded:

- Clear appreciation of the task
- Consistency of **register**
- Clarity of thought and consistency of argument
- Effective illustration
- Quality of your persuasive writing.

Techniques: Speech

- A **speech** is much more formal than a **talk** and therefore a serious, courteous **register** is appropriate.
- Keep your audience in mind at all times. They are in front of you and you must address them at the beginning and frequently throughout your speech.
- Introduce your theme at the outset of the speech.
- Maintain a formal tone throughout your speech, but use humour, **imagery** and **anecdote** to keep it lively and interesting.
- Employ rhetorical devices, such as questions, **triadic structures** and forceful language, to engage your audience.
- Finish your speech with a brief summary of your points and thank your audience for listening to you.

Test yourself

This text is adapted from a short story entitled 'The Parting Gift' in the 2007 collection *Walk the Blue Fields* by Irish writer Claire Keegan. In this story, a young woman spends her last morning in her rural Irish home before emigrating to New York.

from 'The Parting Gift' by Claire Keegan

When sunlight reaches the foot of the dressing table, you get up and look through the suitcase again. It's hot in New York but it may turn cold in winter. All morning the bantam cocks have crowed. It's not something you will miss.

You must dress and wash, polish your shoes. Outside, dew lies on the fields, white and blank as pages. Soon the sun will burn it off. It's a fine day for the hay.

In her bedroom your mother is moving things around, opening and closing doors. You wonder what it will be like for her when you leave. Part of you doesn't care. She talks through the door.

'You'll have a boiled egg?'

'No thanks, Ma.'

'You'll have something?'

'Later on, maybe.'

'I'll put one on for you.'

Downstairs, water spills into the kettle, the bolt slides back. You hear the dogs rush in, the shutters folding. You've always preferred the house in summer: cool feeling in the kitchen, the back door open, scent of the dark wallflowers after rain.

In the bathroom you brush your teeth. The screws in the mirror have rusted, and the glass is cloudy. You look at yourself and you know you have failed the Leaving Cert. The last exam was history and you blanked out on the dates. You confused the methods of warfare, the kings. English was worse. You tried to explain the line about the dancer and the dance.

You go back to the bedroom and take out the passport. You look strange in the photograph, lost. The ticket says you will arrive in Kennedy airport at 12.25, much the same time as you leave. You take one last look around the room: walls papered yellow

Image 1: 2 October 2010 – Chestnut Hill, Massachusetts, USA – Norte Dame Fighting Irish fans

with roses, high ceiling stained where the slate came off, cord of the electric heater swinging out like a tail from under the bed. It used to be an open room at the top of the stairs but Eugene put an end to all of that, got the carpenters in and the partition built, installed the door. You remember him giving you the key, how much that meant to you at the time.

Downstairs, your mother stands over the gas cooker waiting for the pot to boil. You stand at the door and look out. It hasn't rained for days; the spout that runs down from the yard is little more than a trickle. The scent of hay drifts up from neighbouring fields. As soon as the dew burns it off, the Rudd brothers will be out in the meadows turning the rows, saving it while the weather lasts. With pitchforks they'll gather what the baler leaves behind. Mrs Rudd will bring out the flask, the salad. They will lean against the bales and eat their fill. Laughter will carry up the avenue, clear, like birdcall over water.

'It's another fine day.' You feel the need for speech.

Your mother makes some animal sound in her throat. You turn to look at her. She wipes her eyes with the back of her hand. She's never made any allowance for tears.

'Is Eugene up?' she says.

'I don't know. I didn't hear him.'

'I'll go and wake him.'

Narrative WRITING

It's going on for six. Still an hour before you leave. The saucepan boils and you go over to lower the flame. Inside, three eggs knock against each other. One is cracked, a ribbon streaming white. You turn down the gas. You don't like your eggs soft.

Eugene comes down wearing his Sunday clothes. He looks tired. He looks much the same as he always does.

'Well, Sis,' he says. 'Are you all set?'

'Yeah.'

'You have your ticket and everything?'

'I do.'

Your mother puts out the cups and plates, slices a quarter out of the loaf. This knife is old, its teeth worn in places. You eat the bread, drink the tea and wonder what Americans eat for breakfast. Eugene tops his eggs, butters bread, shares it with the dogs. Nobody says anything. When the clock strikes six, Eugene reaches for his cap.

'There's a couple of things I've got to do up the yard,' he says. 'I won't be long.'

Image 2: A group of Irish immigrants on their way to New York, early 1900s

'That's all right.'

'You'd want to leave on time,' your mother says. 'You wouldn't want to get a puncture.'

You place your dirty dishes on the draining board. You have nothing to say to your mother. If you started, you would say the wrong things and you wouldn't want it to end that way. You go upstairs but you'd rather not go back into the room. You stand on the landing. They start talking in the kitchen but you don't hear what they say. A sparrow swoops down onto the window ledge and pecks at his reflection, his beak striking the glass. You watch him until you can't watch him any longer and he flies away.

QUESTION A

(i) Based on your reading of the above text, what impression do you form of the life the young woman is leaving behind? Support your view with reference to the text. (15)

(ii) Which one of the visual images (**1** or **2**) do you think best illustrates the above text? In your response refer to both visual images. (15)

(iii) Identify and comment on **at least three** features of Claire Keegan's writing style in this extract. (20)

QUESTION B

The seasons feature prominently in 'The Parting Gift'. Write **a descriptive passage** on your experience of summer **or** winter while living either at home or abroad. (50)

Narrative WRITING

Novel and modern fairy tale

Introduction

In this unit you will be introduced to two **genres** of **narrative** writing: the novel and the modern fairy tale.

The word '**novel**' comes from the Latin word *novellus*, which means 'new'. A novel is a fictional prose narrative of considerable length that deals imaginatively with human experience through a connected sequence of events involving a group of persons in a specific setting. The genre encompasses a wide range of types and styles, including fantasy, science fiction, crime, romantic, realist and historical novels. Though forerunners of the novel appeared in a number of places, including ancient Rome and eleventh-century Japan, the European novel is usually said to have begun in the early seventeenth century with Miguel de Cervantes's *Don Quixote*. The novel was established as a literary form in English by the eighteenth century.

The typical elements of a conventional novel are plot, character, setting, narrative method and **point of view**. However, writers have always experimented with the novel form. As early as 1759 Laurence Sterne published his now famous experimental novel *Tristram Shandy*, and in the twentieth century writers such as Virginia Woolf and James Joyce were noted for their experimental approach to the novel. A shorter form of the novel is known as a *novella*.

A **fairy tale** is a short story that typically features fantasy characters and elements of magic. The term can also be used to refer to any short story that could not be literally true. Modern fairy stories adapt the features of classic stories, such as *Cinderella*, *Snow White* or *Tom Thumb*, to suit the contemporary world. They are part of a long literary tradition of writing that is not based in reality. Fantasy, fable and myth all belong to this tradition.

Narrative WRITING

READ–ANALYSE–MAKE

Chimamanda Ngozi Adichie is a contemporary Nigerian writer.
Her first novel, *Purple Hibiscus*, received wide critical acclaim.
The short story 'Hair' is an example of a modern fairy tale.

READ

Narrative WRITING

'Hair' by Chimamanda Ngozi Adichie

The mother cried every day. The father had signed the agreement one afternoon after drinking a whole carton of Guinness at the club, after his friend Lugardson proposed a game of cards and wrote out the agreement that said whoever won would take over the other's property and added that it was a joke of course and not at all legal. And so the father signed it and then lost the game. Lugardson took the agreement to court and the judge was Lugardson's crony and he ruled that the father had truly signed away all that he owned. His company. His homes. His cars. He gave the family a week to hand over to Lugardson. The father said, "But it was a joke! The agreement was hastily written on a receipt! It was a joke!" But the judge ignored him. The father fell to the floor and thrashed and wept. Later, he said to the mother, "I thought Lugardson was my friend," and the mother told him to shut up. "Are you stupid? How could he be your friend? He has been waiting for a way to take over your fortune!" And she added that she had often felt Lugardson looking at her in an untoward way, too, which was a lie, but the mother liked to burnish her stories.

The stories she told herself now that she cried every day did not need burnishing, though, because they were true: stories of their old life when they lived in the flower-hugged house on Queens Drive, when all of Lagos worshipped them. Now, none of their friends came to their mice-filled flat where the landlord often removed their electricity meter.

But the mother's greatest shame was her hair. It was matted, with thick clumps of natural undergrowth because relaxers and weaves were now unaffordable. She had been the toast of Lagos with her long and straight perm, and now she always wore a headscarf, even when alone.

The daughter, too, could no longer afford relaxers and so had cut her hair off, and watched in wonder as it grew back, soft and dense like wool, for she had never seen her natural hair. In their old life, as soon as her hair grew out, it had been singed and straightened. Now it was vibrant and kinky and full. She did not comb it but lovingly untangled it every morning with her fingers. The son, who used to work with the father in the company and now spent his days lying around limp with depression, asked that she cover her ugly hair with a scarf. The daughter was close to the son, had done most of his school assignments while he went to the clubs, and she could not understand his calling her hair ugly when it was the only beautiful thing they had left. Just like it was cheap gin that now kept the father going (sometimes he even drank his old bottles of cologne because he said they had alcohol in them), it was her hair, untangling and twisting and glorying in it, that kept her from thinking too much of her constant hunger. She wished that she could reverse their fortune; it was possible only if they could get the agreement itself and take it to a judge who was not corrupt.

One day Lugardson came and said he knew how difficult life had become for them and he wanted to offer one of the children a job; it was the least he could do. Lugardson was a wily man, with a thin mind and thin arms. His benevolence was disgusting. But the father accepted and said the son would take the job. The daughter knew that the father did not even think of considering her; he did not know that she had often done the son's school assignments in the old days.

The son started work and came home to say that he was a mere messenger; he stayed downstairs at the reception and was called only to run errands. But at least he earned a little money and they were able to eat better, although the mother took to vomiting because she could not believe she was now being given mere drops from a river that was rightly hers. An old friend stopped by with some loaves of bread one evening, this a man who used to kneel before the father to beg for money, and said he had heard Lugardson boasting at the club that he kept the agreement in his office to remind himself of the father's stupidity.

The mother told the son that he had to find a way to get the agreement. The son tried different things, the daughter gave him ideas on how to fake his way into the office, but none worked. The son came home in tears. The father sank into deeper depression and began to talk of drinking his urine. The mother cried no longer once but twice a day. Months passed, and then on one hazy day the daughter was untangling her hair, which was now high enough to be held up in a puff like a large rabbit's tail, when she heard the voice. It came from her hair. It was her hair. A voice that sounded like her late grandmother but was somewhat perkier. The agreement is in Lugardson's air conditioner. The daughter shook her head. Then the voice came again. She knew then that there was something magical about her hair, that the delight she felt about it went beyond the mere softness and novelty of it. But knowing it was in his air conditioner was not enough. She needed to know more. And so she began, every morning, to wake up and untangle her hair and wait for the voice. Soon, the voice had told her all that she needed. The agreement was in the air conditioner in his office, stuffed into one of the vents, the place he thought most unlikely for anyone to look. She had to go and get it the next day, at exactly a quarter past noon, and she must stay no longer than 15 minutes in the office or she would be caught.

The daughter set out for Lugardson's office. She got to the gate and lost her nerve. They would never let her in. She was turning back when the voice from her hair told her to walk through, that the gate was open, and she would not be seen. So she did. She walked past the reception and saw the son sitting hunched on a stool. Lugardson's office was empty and smelled oddly of mothballs, and she went right to the air conditioner, stuck her hand into it and pulled an envelope out. Inside was the agreement. Then she heard footsteps; Lugardson was coming. She stared at the door in panic and then began to run her fingers through her hair. Get under the desk. The carpeting was particularly soft under the desk and she settled down and hoped Lugardson would not stay long. He had come in with somebody and was laughing. She checked her watch. Five minutes had passed. Then eight. Lugardson was still talking. Then eleven minutes. She began to sweat. She pushed the envelope into her bra. The person with Lugardson left and Lugardson moved around the office for a while, and his cell phone rang and he answered it and left the office. Thirteen minutes had passed. The daughter flew out from under the desk and began to run as fast as she could, down the stairs, out through the gate, and did not stop until she got to the bus stop.

The father looked at her in shock when she told her story, but it was the mother who took the agreement and held it reverently and then pulled off her scarf and touched her own hair in wonder. The next day they took it to Judge Rotimi, known for being incorruptible, and he ruled that Lugardson give back all he had taken from the father. In addition, Lugardson was to be tried for his crimes. The mother laughed and cried and danced and talked about how she would show pepper to all those nasty people who had deserted her.

The father spoke of ordering cases of champagne. The son, still dazed, suggested they order whisky, too. The daughter watched with joyful amusement, all the time running her fingers through her hair. And they all lived happily ever after.

ANALYSE

Written text

The **exposition** of fairy tales is always dramatic. The usual conventions of setting and character are abandoned as plot is given full attention. In the first paragraph the family lose all their possessions and, although the plot is implausible, the authoritative tone of the narrator allows the reader to suspend disbelief and enter into the world of the story.

Following the exposition, the focus of the fairy tale narrows to a seemingly insignificant detail: the mother's, and then the daughter's, hair. Without money they cannot straighten their hair. The mother feels shame and wears a headscarf while the daughter lovingly discovers her natural hair.

Characters in fairy tales are often described in unusual terms that do not make any literal sense – 'Lugardson was a wily man, with a thin mind' – but somehow the reader understands what is meant. The setting in this story is real: the city of Lagos in Nigeria.

In fairy tales, just at the point when everything seems hopeless, a magical element intervenes. In this case it is a voice in the daughter's hair. The voice tells the daughter exactly where the agreement is in Lugardson's office and when she must get it.

Tension mounts in the latter part of a fairy tale. But just when it seems that everything is lost it suddenly all works out and, in the end, the family 'lived happily ever after'.

It is not possible to explain the full meaning of a fairy tale. This is one of the attractions of the **genre** – they elude rational analysis. At the same time, the reader senses themes very powerfully within fairy tales. In 'Hair' it is clear that gender inequality is an issue. The son is sent to work for Lugardson even though the daughter is obviously cleverer since 'she had often done the son's school assignments in the old days'. Also, the source of salvation in the story is an African woman's hair, something Adichie has talked and written about extensively in political terms.

Visual text

In the Leaving Certificate examination you may be asked to provide a description of a **visual** that you would choose to accompany a written text. For example, imagine that you have been asked to provide a description of a visual that you would choose to accompany the modern fairy tale above.

Narrative WRITING

Think about images associated with fairy tales, such as those by the nineteenth-century French artist Gustave Doré shown below. Then consider the characters, plot and setting of the text and describe a visual from your imagination that combines elements of the **genre** as well as specific details from the text. Remember that, like a written text, visual texts consist of both content and style. Also, the more detail you provide (figures, setting, objects, colour, lighting) the better!

'Sleeping Beauty'

'Little Red Riding-Hood'

MAKE

QUESTION B

Imagine that a celebrity of your choice (writer, sportsperson, musician or actor) has been invited to your school to give a motivational speech to students on the subject of following your dreams. You have been asked to introduce this speaker. Write the text of **the introduction** you would give. (50)

Sample answer

Ladies and gentlemen, teachers and fellow students.

You are assembled here today to listen to the words of someone we all know and admire. Someone who can speak with authority on the subject of daring to have ambition, of not giving in when the going gets tough, of following your dreams.

The person I am speaking of once sat in a school hall, just like you. He studied for the Leaving Certificate, just like you. He thought about the future, just like you. The person I am speaking of had dreams, just like you, and followed those dreams through adversity and anguish to become the success that he is today. Will you be able to say the same about yourself?

The person I am talking about was born in a suburb of Cork city and after secondary school went to UCC to study law. But, a career in law was not his dream. His dream – of treading the

Narrative WRITING

boards – had been ignited when, as a Transition Year student, he had taken part in a drama module. It was a dream that would not go away, a dream that could not be forgotten or abandoned. And so, after much soul-searching, and in spite of the great difficulties attendant on acknowledging to himself and to his family that he had taken a wrong turn in life, this man followed his dream. He left UCC and a legal career behind him and devoted himself instead to acting.

Success followed. From small roles in little-known plays such as *Disco Pigs* to important roles in blockbuster films such as *Inception* and *The Dark Knight* series – this man has done it all. Ladies and gentlemen and fellow students, I give you a man who can truly say that he loves his job, that he has followed his dream: the renowned Irish actor Cillian Murphy.

Techniques: Introducing a speaker

- When introducing a guest speaker, the purpose is to inform the audience of three things: the topic, the topic's relevance to the audience and the speaker's relevance to the topic.
- Begin with yourself: state that you are honoured or delighted to be able to introduce this guest speaker.
- Provide the audience with some of the speaker's credentials, achievements and interesting links to the establishment hosting the speaker.
- Use humour appropriately. Keep the occasion, the audience and the speaker in mind when deciding what is appropriate. Remember that you are there to prepare the audience to receive what the speaker has to say.
- Close your introduction with a clear announcement of the guest speaker's name.

Over to you: Read and analyse

As you read the following text from the 2004 Leaving Certificate exam paper, take note of the annotations in the margins and see if you can isolate the particular words and phrases that the annotations refer to. In this way you will improve your skills in both reading and analysing.

Text 2, 2004: Paul's first day at work

The following text is adapted from the novel *Sons and Lovers*, by D. H. Lawrence, which tells the story of Paul Morel who, in this extract, begins work at Thomas Jordan & Son – suppliers of elasticated stockings. The novel was first published in 1913.

*The **narrative point of view** is <u>omniscient</u>*

On Monday morning, the boy got up at six, to start work. His mother packed his dinner in a small basket, and he set off at a quarter to seven to catch the 7.15 train. Mrs Morel watched him proudly as he trudged over the field. Her elder son, William, was doing well in London and now Paul would be working in Nottingham – her humble contribution to the grandeur of work itself. At eight o'clock Paul climbed the dismal stairs of Jordan's Factory, and stood helplessly against the first great parcel-rack, waiting for somebody to pick him up. Two clerks had arrived before him and were talking in a corner as they took off their coats and rolled up their shirt sleeves. The younger one spied Paul.

Specific details, particularly of time, establish a realistic setting

*Expressive **verb** introduces a sense of drudgery, which will become a recurring **motif***

*The phrase 'the grandeur of work' is an example of **irony***

__Dialogue__ used to create character

"Hello!" he said. "You the new lad? All right, you come on round here."

Paul was led round to a very dark corner.

*Clipped sentences create credible **dialogue***

"You'll be working with Pappleworth," the young man explained. "He's your boss, but he's not come in yet. So you can fetch the letters, if you like, from Mr Melling down there."

The young man pointed to an old clerk in the office.

"All right," said Paul.

"Here's a peg to hang your cap on—here are your entry ledgers—Pappleworth won't be long."

Quotations from letters provide realistic sense of the work environment

Paul sat on a high stool and read some of the letters: "Will you please send me at once a pair of lady's silk, spiral thigh stockings, without feet, such as I had from you last year . . ." or "Major Chamberlain wishes to repeat his previous order for a silk, non-elastic bandage."

*Word choice, clipped **dialogue** and repeated references to time create an almost military atmosphere*

He nervously awaited the arrival of his 'boss' and suffered tortures of shyness when, at half past eight, the factory girls for upstairs trooped past him. Mr Pappleworth arrived at twenty to nine.

*Only the **protagonist**, Paul, is given an interior life (emotions and thoughts)*

"You my new lad?" he said. "Fetched the letters?"

"Yes."

"Copied 'em?"

"No."

Mr Pappleworth sat down beside him, seized the letters, snatched a long entry book out of a rack in front of him, flung it open, seized a pen, and said: "Now look here—you want to copy these letters in here. Think you can do it all right?"

"Yes."

"All right then—let's see you."

*Pappleworth is brought to life not just by his voice, but by his actions – note the revealing choice of **verbs** to describe them*

Narrative WRITING

Paul rather liked copying the letters, but he wrote slowly, laboriously, and exceedingly badly. He was doing the fourth letter and feeling quite busy and happy, when Mr Pappleworth reappeared.

*Three **adverbs** stress Paul's toiling*

Colloquial expressions add colour to the character of Pappleworth and punctuation is used to capture his brusque manner

"Strike my bob, lad, but you're a beautiful writer!" he exclaimed **satirically**. "How many h'yer done? Only three! I'd 'a eaten 'em. Come on, my lad, oh, come on . . . Polly will be crying out for them orders. Here—come out. You'd better watch me do it."

Paul watched the weird little drawings of legs and thighs and ankles which his chief made upon the yellow paper. Mr Pappleworth finished and jumped up.

*Energetic **verbs** perfectly describe Pappleworth's brisk, business-like manner*

Effective use of descriptive detail

"Come with me," he said as he dashed through a door, down some stairs and into the basement where a little group of girls, nicely dressed and in white aprons, stood talking together.

"Have you nothing else to do but talk?" said Mr Pappleworth.

"Only wait for you," said one handsome girl, laughing.

Relationship between self-important Pappleworth and mischievous girls perfectly captured in a single exchange

"Come on then, Paul," said Mr Pappleworth handing over the orders.

"See you later, Paul," said one of the girls.

*Striking **auditory** image*

There was a titter of laughter. Paul went out, blushing deeply, not having spoken a word.

Later, at one o'clock, Paul, feeling very lost, took his dinner basket down into the stack room in the basement, which had the long table on trestles, and ate his meal hurriedly, alone in that cellar of gloom and desolation. At five o'clock all the men went down to the same dungeon and there they had tea, eating bread and butter on the bare dirty boards, talking with the same kind of ugly haste and slovenliness with which they ate their meal. After tea, work went more briskly. Paul made out invoices and prepared his stack of parcels for the post. When the postman finally came everything slacked off and Paul took his dinner basket and, wondering if every work day would be like this, ran to catch the 8.20 train. The day in the factory was just twelve hours long.

Metaphor of prison evokes atmosphere of confinement

*Effective use of descriptive **adjectives***

*Ends on a note of **irony***

Answer the following Leaving Certificate questions using the guidelines below.

Narrative WRITING

QUESTION A

(i) What impression do you get of Paul's workplace from reading the above passage? Support your answer by reference to the text. (15)

(ii) How would you describe the attitudes of the other workers (including Mr Pappleworth) to Paul, the new arrival at Jordan's Factory? Illustrate your answer by reference to the text. (15)

(iii) What advice would you give to the management of Jordan's Factory about how they might improve working conditions for new employees like Paul? (20)

Answer guidelines

Part (i): begin by explicitly answering the question; for instance, *I get a strong impression of Paul's workplace from reading the passage*. You may base your impression on the content and/or the language of the extract. You are free to find Paul's workplace attractive or unattractive, or a combination of the two. Possible points include: physical surroundings are dark, gloomy, dismal; attractive/unattractive nature of the work and the factory-like environment; the banter of the workers; co-workers are friendly and supportive, or demanding, or critical of Paul.

Part (ii): begin by explicitly answering the question; for instance, *A variety of attitudes are displayed by the other workers to Paul, the new arrival at Jordan's Factory*. Reference to Pappleworth is optional. You may elect to focus on the other workers, such as the clerks or the girls. Possible points include: clerks are friendly, helpful, cheerful; Pappleworth is patronising but avuncular and supporting; girls are forward, teasing.

Part (iii): begin by answering the question; for instance, *I would give strong advice to the management of Jordan's Factory about how they might improve working conditions for new employees like Paul*. Any suggestions reasonably inferred from the working conditions or atmosphere described in the text are acceptable. Reference to modern management approaches and technology (such as computers) is allowed. Possible points include: more advance information about the job requirements or the nature of the work; introduction to other staff members; attention given to the physical environs of the workplace.

Over to you: Make

In this unit a student exemplar of a Leaving Certificate Question B task requiring textual intervention is provided as an extra helping hand. It is followed by a similar Question B task.

QUESTION B

Imagine that Mr Pappleworth is asked, on the basis of Paul's first day at work, to write **a report** giving his impressions of Paul Morel as an employee. Write the text of his report. (50)

Student exemplar: Report on Paul Morel

Based on the lad's debut into the working world, I am very pleased with the result. He arrived promptly and was suitably attired. He immediately struck me as superior to his predecessor, the distasteful, incompetent ragamuffin, Grimshaw.

The boy is a gangly lad, barely sixteen, but his frame has little effect on his eagerness and his willingness to please and to work. However, he still needs some further getting used to the workings of Thomas Jordan and Sons.

I instructed the boy in the procedures for copying letter orders and in the preparation of invoices and parcels for shipping. He grasped these tasks quickly and needed no further instructions prior to my initial 'shove-off'. However he does write terribly slowly and this will be his downfall on busier days when shipments are flying his way. This, added to by the torture and teasing that factory girls can administer, may make this shy boy flustered. All the same, he couldn't possibly make a worse mess of things than that unsavoury reprobate, Grimshaw.

As for the boy's shyness, he barely spoke today, except for the odd "Yes, sir, No, sir, Excuse me, sir", which I found rather amusing, but I was also taken aback by his extreme politeness – how nice to see such respect for an elder and occupational superior in today's world of Jack Grimshaws. He's a credit to his mother. Perhaps in a few days the lad will settle into his surroundings and we'll be able to extract some complete sentences from him.

All in all I am rather pleased with the boy's first day and feel that he will do well in Thomas Jordan and Sons, and perhaps within a year or two he may be sufficiently knowledgeable of the elasticated stocking industry to gain promotion to the level of clerk.

Techniques: Textual intervention

- Some of the Leaving Certificate Question B tasks invite students to engage in textual intervention. There are many ways to 'intervene' in a text; for example, you might create an alternative ending, transform a **narrative** text into drama or perhaps write a **parody** of a text. However, in the Leaving Certificate examination, students are usually invited to take on the persona of a character from one of the texts printed on the paper and then create a new text, such as a **diary** or report, in the voice of this character.

- Marks are awarded to students who engage wholeheartedly with the task by adopting the personality, accent and **colloquialisms** of the character in question.

- The above 'Report on Paul Morel', supposedly written by Mr Pappleworth, is an excellent example of textual intervention as the writer has not only successfully adopted the persona of Mr Pappleworth, but also extended the narrative beyond the confines of the text by introducing the fictional character of Grimshaw.

Now answer the following Leaving Certificate question using the techniques demonstrated above and the tips given below.

QUESTION B

Imagine that you are Paul Morel. Write **the diary entry** that you would make following your first day at work in Thomas Jordan & Son. (50)

Narrative WRITING

Answer tips

Write in a style broadly suited to a personal diary. Evidence of the following will be rewarded:

- Clear appreciation of the task
- Consistency of **register**
- Good use of evidence available in the text.

Test yourself

This text is adapted from the opening of *The Picture of Dorian Gray*, a novel by the Irish playwright and poet Oscar Wilde, published in 1890. In this extract the artist Basil Hallward discusses with his friend Lord Henry Wotton a portrait that he has painted of a beautiful young man.

from *The Picture of Dorian Gray* by Oscar Wilde

The studio was filled with the rich odour of roses, and when the light summer wind stirred amidst the trees of the garden, there came through the open door the heavy scent of the lilac, or the more delicate perfume of the pink-flowering thorn.

From the corner of the divan of Persian saddle-bags on which he was lying, smoking, as was his custom, innumerable cigarettes, Lord Henry Wotton could just catch the gleam of the honey-sweet and honey-coloured blossoms of a laburnum, whose tremulous branches seemed hardly able to bear the burden of a beauty so flame-like as theirs; and now and then the fantastic shadows of birds in flight flitted across the long tussore-silk curtains that were stretched in front of the huge window, producing a kind of momentary Japanese effect, and making him think of those pallid, jade-faced painters of Tokyo who, through the medium of an art that is necessarily immobile, seek to convey the sense of swiftness and motion. The sullen murmur of the bees shouldering their way through the long unmown grass, or circling with monotonous insistence round the dusty gilt horns of the straggling woodbine, seemed to make the stillness more oppressive. The dim roar of London was like the bourdon note of a distant organ.

In the centre of the room, clamped to an upright easel, stood the full-length portrait of a young man of extraordinary personal beauty, and in front of it, some little distance away, was sitting the artist himself, Basil Hallward, whose sudden disappearance some years ago caused, at the time, such public excitement and gave rise to so many strange conjectures.

As the painter looked at the gracious and comely form he had so skilfully mirrored in his art, a smile of pleasure passed across his face, and seemed about to linger there. But he suddenly started up, and closing his eyes, placed his fingers upon the lids, as though he sought to imprison within his brain some curious dream from which he feared he might awake.

"It is your best work, Basil, the best thing you have ever done," said Lord Henry languidly. "You must certainly send it next year to the Grosvenor. The Academy is too large and too vulgar. Whenever I have gone there, there have been either so many people that I have not been able to see the pictures, which was dreadful, or so many pictures that I have not been able to see the people, which was worse. The Grosvenor is really the only place."

Narrative WRITING

139

"I don't think I shall send it anywhere," he answered, tossing his head back in that odd way that used to make his friends laugh at him at Oxford. "No, I won't send it anywhere."

Lord Henry elevated his eyebrows and looked at him in amazement through the thin blue wreaths of smoke that curled up in such fanciful whorls from his heavy, opium-tainted cigarette. "Not send it anywhere? My dear fellow, why? Have you any reason? What odd chaps you painters are! You do anything in the world to gain a reputation. As soon as you have one, you seem to want to throw it away. It is silly of you, for there is only one thing in the world worse than being talked about, and that is not being talked about. A portrait like this would set you far above all the young men in England, and make the old men quite jealous, if old men are ever capable of any emotion."

"I know you will laugh at me," he replied, "but I really can't exhibit it. I have put too much of myself into it."

Lord Henry stretched himself out on the divan and laughed.

"Yes, I knew you would; but it is quite true, all the same."

"Too much of yourself in it! Upon my word, Basil, I didn't know you were so vain; and I really can't see any resemblance between you, with your rugged strong face and your coal-black hair, and this young Adonis, who looks as if he was made out of ivory and rose-leaves. Why, my dear Basil, he is a Narcissus, and you—well, of course you have an intellectual expression and all that. But beauty, real beauty, ends where an intellectual expression begins. Intellect is in itself a mode of exaggeration, and destroys the harmony of any face. The moment one sits down to think, one becomes all nose, or all forehead, or something horrid. Look at the successful men in any of the learned professions. How perfectly hideous they are!"

QUESTION A

(i)   Would you consider the above passage an effective opening for a novel? Give reasons for your answer, supporting your views with close reference to the text. (15)

(ii) Based on your reading of the above text, what impression do you form of the character Lord Henry Wotton? Support your view with reference to the text. (15)

(iii) Identify **at least three** features of Oscar Wilde's writing style in the text and comment on their effectiveness. (20)

QUESTION B

Imagine that a well-known artist is coming to your school to talk about his or her life and work. You have been asked to write a report for the visitor in which you give a descriptive account of your school and its locality. Write the text of the **report** you would prepare. (50)

Short story

Introduction

The **short story** is one of the main composition types set on the Leaving Certificate paper.

A short story is a limited piece of fiction. Determining what exactly separates a short story from longer fictional formats is problematic, but a classic definition of a short story is that one should be able to read it in one sitting.

Many short stories conform to the traditional elements of dramatic structure:

- **Exposition**: introduction of setting, situation and main characters
- Complication: event that brings conflict into the situation
- **Climax**: point of highest tension in terms of the conflict
- Resolution: point when the conflict finds some resolution, for good or ill, as far the characters are concerned.

Not all short stories conform to this pattern. For example, modern short stories only occasionally have an exposition (more typically beginning in the middle of the action) and the endings are often abrupt and open-ended. Usually, however, a short story focuses on one incident; has a single plot, a single setting and a small number of characters; and covers a short period of time.

When writing a short story, focus on a little corner of life. Beware of overlong introductions. Remember that it *is* a story and should contain some plot, some happening or progression of some sort. This will usually mean tension or conflict and a resolution of that conflict. In a Leaving Certificate short story, however, plot should be kept to a minimum, as the more important elements are:

- **Characterisation**: reveal your characters through description, **dialogue** and actions; go for a little depth and difference to make your characters credible
- Setting: use the senses – feel it, see it, smell it.

It is essential to keep your story relevant to the title – don't wander off and then try to force it round at the very end.

Narrative WRITING

Techniques: Short story

- Shape your story around one or two characters. Describe the characters in terms of their appearance, but more importantly, show them as living beings – using body language, facial expression, gesture, action and so on.

  > Be sure not to discuss your hero's state of mind. Make it clear from his actions.
  > Anton Chekhov, Russian writer, 1860–1904

- Setting creates the atmosphere of the story, and so should be given careful consideration. Bring your setting to life by providing specific detail and through the use of the senses. Employ **visual**, **auditory**, **tactile**, **olfactory** and **gustatory imagery**.

  > Everyone has to be somewhere.
  > Spike Milligan, writer, of English and Irish parentage, 1918–2002

- In a Leaving Certificate short story, plot needs to be simple in order to work. Placing a character in a situation of conflict (external or internal), where a choice must be made, is a good strategy. Also, keep the structure of your story simple: either chronological or **flashback**. In general, it works better to write your short story in the past tense.

  > I don't praise plots as accurate representations of life but ways to keep readers reading.
  > Kurt Vonnegut, American writer, 1922–2007

- Include **dialogue** in your story. Voice is a useful tool for revealing character. Use **colloquial** language, carefully chosen words and tone of voice to create effective dialogue. In terms of presentation, remember that you need a new line for every new speaker and that you should indent each speech by beginning a few spaces in from the left-hand margin.

  > Writing good dialogue is art as well as craft.
  > Stephen King, American writer, born 1947

- You can use first person, second person, third person or omniscient **point of view**. Remember, who tells the story greatly influences the story.

  > The choice of the point of view from which the story is told is arguably the most important single decision that the writer has to make, for it fundamentally affects the way readers will respond, emotionally and morally, to the fictional characters and their actions.
  > David Lodge, English writer, born 1935

- The most important element of a short story is that it moves towards some kind of change within your main character. This change may be attitudinal (thinking differently), emotional (feeling differently) or circumstantial (going to do something differently). The sudden and intense sensation of change experienced by a character in a story is known as an **epiphany**.

  > Find the key emotion; this may be all you need know to find your short story.
  > F. Scott Fitzgerald, American writer, 1896–1940

Narrative WRITING

- Use **pathetic fallacy** in your resolution to add depth. This is a technique whereby descriptions of the external world are used to economically convey mood and atmosphere.

> I know of only one rule: style cannot be too clear, too simple.
>
> Stendhal, French writer, 1783–1842

READ–ANALYSE–MAKE: Short Story One

John Cheever, an American novelist and short story writer, was one of the most important short fiction writers of the twentieth century. In 'Reunion', first published in 1962, a boy named Charlie recalls his final meeting in New York City with his father, an alcoholic, who is unnamed.

'Reunion' by John Cheever

The last time I saw my father was in Grand Central Station. I was going from my grandmother's in the Adirondacks to a cottage on the Cape that my mother had rented, and I wrote my father that I would be in New York between trains for an hour and a half, and asked if we could have lunch together. His secretary wrote to say that he would meet me at the information booth at noon, and at twelve o'clock sharp I saw him coming through the crowd. He was a stranger to me—my mother divorced him three years ago and I hadn't seen him since—but as soon as I saw him I felt that he was my father, my flesh and blood, my future and my doom. I knew that when I was grown I would be something like him; I would have to plan my campaigns within his limitations. He was a big, good-looking man, and I was terribly happy to see him again. He struck me on the back and shook my hand. 'Hi, Charlie,' he said. 'Hi, boy. I'd like to take you up to my club, but it's in the Sixties, and if you have to catch an early train I guess we'd better get something to eat around here.' He put his arm around me, and I smelled my father the way my mother sniffs a rose. It was a rich compound of whiskey, after-shave lotion, shoe polish, woollens, and the rankness of the mature male. I hoped that someone would see us together. I wished that we could be photographed. I wanted some record of our having been together.

We went out of the station and up a side street to a restaurant. It was still early, and the place was empty. The bartender was quarrelling with a delivery boy, and there was one very old waiter in a red coat down by the kitchen door. We sat down, and my father hailed the waiter in a loud voice. '*Kellner!*' he shouted. '*Garçon! Cameriere! You!*' His boisterousness in the empty restaurant seemed out of place. 'Could we have a little service here!' he shouted. 'Chop-chop.' Then he clapped his hands. This caught the waiter's attention, and he shuffled over to our table.

'Were you clapping your hands at me?' he asked.

'Calm down, calm down, *sommelier*,' my father said. 'If it isn't too much to ask of you – if it wouldn't be above and beyond the call of duty, we would like a couple of Beefeater Gibsons.'

'I don't like to be clapped at,' the waiter said.

'I should have brought my whistle,' my father said. 'I have a whistle that is audible only to the ears of old waiters. Now, take out your little pad and your little pencil and see if you can get this straight: two Beefeater Gibsons. Repeat after me: two Beefeater Gibsons.'

'I think you'd better go somewhere else,' the waiter said quietly.

'That,' said my father, 'is one of the most brilliant suggestions I have ever heard. Come on, Charlie, let's get the hell out of here.'

I followed my father out of that restaurant into another. He was not so boisterous this time. Our drinks came, and he cross-questioned me about the baseball season. He then struck the edge of his empty glass with his knife and began shouting again. '*Garçon! Kellner! Cameriere! You!* Could we trouble you to bring us two more of the same.'

'How old is the boy?' the waiter asked.

'That,' my father said, 'is none of your God-damned business.'

'I'm sorry, sir,' the waiter said, 'but I won't serve the boy another drink.'

'Well, I have some news for you,' my father said. 'I have some very interesting news for you. This doesn't happen to be the only restaurant in New York. They've opened another on the corner. Come on, Charlie.'

He paid the bill, and I followed him out of the restaurant into another. Here the waiters wore pink jackets like hunting coats, and there was a lot of horse tack on the walls. We sat down, and my father began to shout again.

'Master of the hounds! Tallyhoo and all that sort of thing. We'd like a little something in the way of a stirrup cup. Namely, two Bibson Geefeaters.'

'Two Bibson Geefeaters?' the waiter asked, smiling.

'You know damned well what I want,' my father said angrily. 'I want two Beefeater Gibsons, and make it snappy. Things have changed in jolly old England. So my friend the duke tells me. Let's see what England can produce in the way of a cocktail.'

'This isn't England,' the waiter said.

'Don't argue with me,' my father said. 'Just do as you're told.'

'I just thought you might like to know where you are,' the waiter said.

'If there is one thing I cannot tolerate,' my father said, 'it is an impudent domestic. Come on, Charlie.'

The fourth place we went to was Italian. '*Buon giorno*,' my father said. '*Per favore, possiamo avere due cocktail americani, forti, forti. Molto gin, poco vermut.*'

'I don't understand Italian,' the waiter said.

'Oh, come off it,' my father said. 'You understand Italian, and you know damned well you do. *Vogliamo due cocktail americani. Subito.*'

The waiter left us and spoke with the captain, who came over to our table and said, 'I'm sorry, sir, but this table is reserved.'

'All right,' my father said. 'Get us another table.'

'All the tables are reserved,' the captain said.

'I get it,' my father said. 'You don't desire our patronage. Is that it? Well, the hell with you. *Vada all'inferno.* Let's go, Charlie.'

'I have to get my train,' I said.

'I'm sorry, sonny,' my father said. 'I'm terribly sorry.' He put his arm around me and pressed me against him. 'I'll walk you back to the station. If there had only been time to go up to my club.'

'That's all right, Daddy,' I said.

'I'll get you a paper,' he said. 'I'll get you a paper to read on the train.'

Then he went up to a news stand and said, 'Kind sir, will you be good enough to favour me with one of your God-damned, no-good, ten-cent afternoon papers?' The clerk turned away from him and stared at a magazine cover. 'Is it asking too much, kind sir,' my father said, 'is it asking too much for you to sell me one of your disgusting specimens of yellow journalism?'

'I have to go, Daddy,' I said. 'It's late.'

'Now, just wait a second, sonny,' he said. 'Just wait a second. I want to get a rise out of this chap.'

'Goodbye, Daddy,' I said, and I went down the stairs and got my train, and that was the last time I saw my father.

ANALYSE

This story is told in first person **point of view** by a boy named Charlie who meets his father for the first time in three years. The **narrative** describes a single situation, but the incident in question encapsulates an entire lifetime: 'I knew that when I was grown I would be something like him'.

In the **exposition** the boy is clearly looking forward to meeting his father. It is a significant occasion for him. But already there are ominous signs, for example the response from the father is business-like and impersonal: 'His secretary wrote to say . . . at twelve o'clock sharp I saw him coming through the crowd.' As in all good writing, the character is *shown* to the reader and *not told* to the reader.

Tension is created in the story through conflict. Just as the narrator experiences joy at the meeting with his father, the reader becomes aware of potential difficulties. The boy is in a situation we know is going to disappoint him, although he is unaware of that. The character of the father is presented primarily through **dialogue**. The choice of words and sarcastic tone of voice are revealing: 'I should have brought my whistle.'

Remember, an essential technique in good short story writing is show, don't tell. Throughout the story the boy's reactions and feelings are not analysed and explained, but shown, through actions and responses: 'I followed my father out of that restaurant into another.' Small but significant gestures also create the character of the father: 'He then struck the edge of his empty glass with his knife'; as do the reactions of others to the father: 'The clerk turned away from him and stared at a magazine cover.'

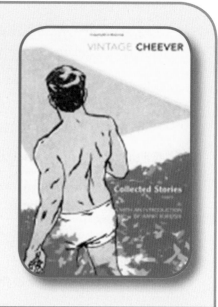

The resolution of the story offers no analysis, explanation or reflection. Interpretation is left to the reader: 'that was the last time I saw my father'.

MAKE

Write the **interior monologue** of a character sitting in a restaurant waiting for someone to arrive. Use the techniques below as a helping hand and, if you like, read the exemplar for inspiration!

Exemplar: Waiting

Susan is late. The menu is dog-eared and peeling apart. Kind of depressing, really. The ceiling is too low, too heavily plastered. The light is dim. I can barely see the movement of that second hand flinching its way around the face of my watch. Cool, constant face. Susan is ten minutes late. The walls of the room are red. Red? Maybe Susan will wear that red dress she bought in London. Matches her lipstick. Waiters never stop flitting around. Look at that one arranging the forks and the spoons. The way they clink softly every time they meet. Is it a game? Now he's folding a paper serviette into a fan. Looks ridiculous. Wax dripping from a candle onto the table. Droplets of condensation rolling down the outside of the wine bottle. Better check the watch again. Twenty minutes late. Where the hell is she?

Techniques: Interior monologue

- An **interior monologue** is a valuable technique in **characterisation**. It is a way of seeing into a character's mind: what he or she thinks, feels, believes and so on. Don't, therefore, waste monologue on simply reporting facts.
- People do not think in a clear and logical way. Instead, thinking is an extremely complex and random activity, and you should attempt to show this in some way.
- A monologue is a combination of observation of the external world and expression of the interior world including, for example, feelings, attitudes and preoccupations.

Narrative Writing

READ–ANALYSE–MAKE: Short Story Two

Gabriel García Márquez is a Columbian novelist, short story writer and journalist. His works have achieved significant critical acclaim, most notably for popularising a literary style known as **magic realism**, a **genre** in which magic events are a natural part of an otherwise ordinary environment. The following short story, 'One of These Days', was first published in 1962.

READ

'One of These Days' by Gabriel García Márquez

Monday dawned warm and rainless. Aurelio Escovar, a dentist without a degree, and a very early riser, opened his office at six. He took some false teeth, still mounted in their plaster mould, out of the glass case and put on the table a fistful of instruments which he arranged in size order, as if they were on display. He wore a collarless striped shirt, closed at the neck with a golden stud, and pants held up by suspenders. He was erect and skinny, with a look that rarely corresponded to the situation, the way deaf people have of looking.

When he had things arranged on the table, he pulled the drill toward the dental chair and sat down to polish the false teeth. He seemed not to be thinking about what he was doing, but worked steadily, pumping the drill with his feet, even when he didn't need it.

After eight he stopped for a while to look at the sky through the window, and he saw two <u>pensive</u> buzzards who were drying themselves in the sun on the ridgepole of the house next door. He went on working with the idea that before lunch it would rain again. The shrill voice of his eleven-year-old son interrupted his concentration.

'Papa.'

'What?'

'The Mayor wants to know if you'll pull his tooth.'

'Tell him I'm not here.'

He was polishing a gold tooth. He held it at arm's length, and examined it with his eyes half closed. His son shouted again from the little waiting room.

'He says you are, too, because he can hear you.'

The dentist kept examining the tooth. Only when he had put it on the table with the finished work did he say:

'So much the better.'

He operated the drill again. He took several pieces of a bridge out of a cardboard box where he kept the things he still had to do and began to polish the gold.

'Papa.'

Narrative WRITING

'What?'

He still hadn't changed his expression.

'He says if you don't take out his tooth, he'll shoot you.'

Without hurrying, with an extremely tranquil movement, he stopped pedaling the drill, pushed it away from the chair, and pulled the lower drawer of the table all the way out. There was a revolver. 'O.K.,' he said. 'Tell him to come and shoot me.'

He rolled the chair over opposite the door, his hand resting on the edge of the drawer. The Mayor appeared at the door. He had shaved the left side of his face, but the other side, swollen and in pain, had a five-day-old beard. The dentist saw many nights of desperation in his dull eyes. He closed the drawer with his fingertips and said softly:

'Sit down.'

'Good morning,' said the Mayor.

'Morning,' said the dentist.

While the instruments were boiling, the Mayor leaned his skull on the headrest of the chair and felt better. His breath was icy. It was a poor office: an old wooden chair, the pedal drill, a glass case with ceramic bottles. Opposite the chair was a window with a shoulder-high cloth curtain. When he felt the dentist approach, the Mayor braced his heels and opened his mouth.

Aurelio Escovar turned his head toward the light. After inspecting the infected tooth, he closed the Mayor's jaw with a cautious pressure of his fingers.

'It has to be without anesthesia,' he said.

'Why?'

'Because you have an abscess.'

The Mayor looked him in the eye. 'All right,' he said, and tried to smile. The dentist did not return the smile. He brought the basin of sterilized instruments to the worktable and took them out of the water with a pair of cold tweezers, still without hurrying. Then he pushed the spittoon with the tip of his shoe, and went to wash his hands in the washbasin. He did all this without looking at the Mayor. But the Mayor didn't take his eyes off him.

It was a lower wisdom tooth. The dentist spread his feet and grasped the tooth with the hot forceps. The Mayor seized the arms of the chair, braced his feet with all his strength, and felt an icy void in his kidneys, but didn't make a sound. The dentist moved only his wrist. Without rancour, rather with a bitter tenderness, he said:

'Now you'll pay for our twenty dead men.'

The Mayor felt the crunch of bones in his jaw, and his eyes filled with tears. But he didn't breathe until he felt the tooth come out. Then he saw it through his tears. It seemed so foreign to his pain that he failed to understand his torture of the five previous nights.

Bent over the spittoon, sweating, panting, he unbuttoned his tunic and reached for the handkerchief in his pants pocket. The dentist gave him a clean cloth.

'Dry your tears,' he said.

The Mayor did. He was trembling. While the dentist washed his hands, he saw the crumbling ceiling and a dusty spider web with spider's eggs and dead insects. The dentist returned, drying his hands. 'Go to bed,' he said, 'and gargle with salt water.' The Mayor stood up, said goodbye with a casual military salute, and walked toward the door, stretching his legs, without buttoning up his tunic.

'Send the bill,' he said.

'To you or the town?'

The Mayor didn't look at him. He closed the door and said through the screen:

'It's the same damn thing.'

ANALYSE

The story's opening establishes a simple but atmospheric setting: it is a warm and rainless Monday morning in the office of a dentist 'without a degree'. This last detail is telling, as it conjures a world that exists beyond the usual rule of law. Márquez shows the character as the dentist goes about his work in a slow and methodical manner. Coupled with **visual** description, this creates a strong impression of the character of the dentist. In the third paragraph Márquez uses a **symbolic** image of buzzards to signal to the reader that the theme of this story is menace.

The mayor arrives and wishes to have his tooth pulled. He threatens violence if the dentist will not see him. Eventually the dentist lets him in, examines him, and then removes the infected wisdom tooth without anaesthesia. Márquez conveys the mayor's pain in carefully chosen **verbs** ('seized the arms of the chair', 'braced his feet') and in memorable **sensory imagery** ('felt an icy void in his kidneys, but didn't make a sound'). We realise that the dentist has deliberately made the mayor suffer when he says, 'Now you'll pay for our twenty dead men.' Márquez depicts an intense power struggle in this tale of manipulation.

The entire drama is played out in clipped exchanges of **dialogue** and shown through body language and action. The dentist is not a powerful man (he is not wealthy and his office is poorly supplied); the mayor is the epitome of corrupt, even murderous, political power. But the situation reverses this hierarchy, placing the mayor at the dentist's mercy. The reversal is profound, but temporary, for as soon as the mayor has recovered he tells the dentist to send on the bill. When the dentist asks whether to send it 'To you or the town?' the mayor replies, 'It's the same damn thing.'

As the title, 'One of These Days', implies, the dentist has learned something about power, but the conclusion of the story is open-ended. The final **symbol**, 'dusty spider web with spider's eggs and dead insects', brilliantly evokes the atmosphere of death and violence that hangs over the world of this story.

Narrative WRITING

Write **a resolution to a short story** on the theme of conflict. Use **pathetic fallacy** to convey mood and atmosphere. Use the techniques below as a helping hand and, if you like, read the exemplar for inspiration!

Exemplar: Conflict

They finished their tea in silence. As Mairéad walked back to the car she felt a strange loss, a disappointment she couldn't quite place. The wheat in the far field had lost its golden colour and looked dull in the fading light. The rain had been and gone but the clouds were still low and puddles on the driveway had trapped the silver moonlight in them. On the cold breeze Mairéad caught the scent of withered roses and, for a moment, she almost cried.

Techniques: Resolution

- While there are no rules on how to write a successful short story, it is helpful to have some understanding of how the best short stories end – this is never with a neat tying up of all loose ends or a dramatic cliffhanger or someone waking up from a dream.
- Among the most effective devices for ending a short story is **pathetic fallacy**. Pathetic fallacy is a literary term for the attributing of human emotion to nature; for example, when clouds are sullen, when leaves dance, when dogs laugh or when rocks seem indifferent. Ending your short story with pathetic fallacy will allow you to both illustrate the mood of your central character and create an open-ended atmospheric resolution.

Exam tips for short stories

As you will note from the instructions to Leaving Certificate correctors and the extracts from the Chief Examiner's Report in 2008 reproduced below, the better stories were original and even inspiring, with good development of plot and character. An awareness of **narrative** shape (that is, **exposition**, **climax**, resolution) is highly rewarded in the short story. Conversely, less successful attempts struggle with credible **characterisation**, reveal limited awareness of narrative shape or rely on adapting unconvincing stories to satisfy the requirements of the task, and are penalised accordingly.

Instructions to correctors in the marking schemes of Leaving Certificate 2008–2012 short story compositions

2008

Question 3: '. . . 17-year-old male **protagonist** with a darting gaze . . .' Write a short story in which the central character is a rebellious teenager (male or female).

Instruction to correctors: Reward awareness of the narrative shape of a short story. The character of the rebellious teenager should be central to the storyline.

Chief Examiner's remarks: This was by far the most popular choice. The better stories were original and even inspiring, with good development of plot and character. Less successful attempts struggled with credible characterisation and revealed limited awareness of narrative shape.

Question 7: '. . . my camp, my small launch, my treehouse.' Write a short story in which setting/ location is a significant feature.

Instruction to correctors: Reward awareness of the narrative shape of a short story. The setting/ location should be central to the storyline.

Chief Examiner's remarks: Some candidates lacked confidence in handling the setting/location element. While there were fine examples of creative narrative writing, other attempts relied on adapting unconvincing stories to satisfy the requirements of the task.

2009

Question 3: '. . . the decisive moment . . .' Write a short story in which the central character is faced with making an important decision.

Instruction to correctors: Reward awareness of the narrative shape of a short story. The decision facing the central character should play an important part in the storyline.

2010

Question 7: 'What a strange meeting!' Write a short story in which two unusual or eccentric characters meet for the first time.

Instruction to correctors: Reward awareness of the narrative shape of a short story, but expect an encounter between two unusual/eccentric characters. Interpret the terms 'unusual or eccentric' and 'first time' liberally.

2011

Question 3: '. . . the waiting had been magical . . .' Write a story to be included in a collection of modern fairytales.

Instruction to correctors: Reward awareness of the narrative shape of a story. Interpret the term 'modern fairytale' liberally, but expect some element of the fairytale.

2012

Question 7: 'When I was eighteen, I couldn't wait to get out of that town . . .' Write a short story in which a young character is eager to leave home.

Instruction to correctors: Reward awareness of the narrative shape of a short story. The young character's eagerness to leave home should be central to the story.

Narrative WRITING

READ–ANALYSE–MAKE

Read the short story below, written by a sixth-year student in response to the task:

'The door locked behind her . . .'

Write a short story in which power and authority in the household are a central theme.

Student exemplar: Household

Peter walked into the bedroom as the sun eased itself below the horizon. The light glided in through the windows and made the peach walls a warm orange. The loud click of the Brown Thomas loafers dulled to a soft patter as they moved onto the rug. Peter sat on the bed. The mattress sighed under his weight. He slipped off his shoes. He rose again and walked to the wardrobe and opened it. The dark door swung open with the slight creak that accompanies old age. While opening the knot on his tie, Peter gazed out the old bay windows. When he'd bought the house the west-facing window allowed no rude sunlight to break through the blinds on weekend mornings. Now the setting sun serenaded his day.

Nearly twenty-five years had passed since then. A quarter of a century. He smiled. All that time and Peter had never grown tired of that sunset, no matter how exhausted he was.

He slipped off his Adolfo Dominguez watch. He placed it on the marble mantle of the fireplace that hadn't been used in his lifetime. In the process of removing his jacket, Peter paused.

His shadow crept further up the wall as the sun continued its descent.

He had noticed something different. A change that one doesn't expect in a routine such as his. Shrugging his jacket back on, he swivelled on the ball of his left foot. His gaze ran up and down the length of the mantle. He focused in turn on the boxes of custom pens he'd been awarded, the chequebook, the mug covered in pink elephants that contained odds and ends, the spot for his watch and wedding ring, his tin box of change and the plastic bank bags behind it. His eyes searched back and forth, looking for the source of his unease. With the light fading and his nerves beginning to fray, his gaze fell on the box of change. The notes he had half-tucked beneath it were gone.

Peter sighed and removed his jacket. The notes were the pocket money he had intended giving to his son, John, that evening. Thursday nights he gave the boy his weekly allowance. Recently John had been getting into trouble in school and letting his grades slip and Peter had threatened to cut off his allowance, but it was an empty threat, and he hadn't intended carrying it through. Peter opened his shirt buttons as the sky turned red behind him. John had taken the money. Peter knew it.

The top step creaked. The sound of John's footfall on the landing drifted into the room. Peter's fingers hovered over the door handle, before he quickly reached a decision and whisked the door open. John immediately did a double take. He stopped in the shadow of his father. The index finger of his right hand traced small circles over the pocket of his jeans. The dying rays of sunlight peered over Peter's shoulder and shone into John's eyes. The landing seemed to darken despite the new source of light.

'Looking for your pocket money?' Peter asked.

John's right hand clenched into a fist while his eyes found interest in the lower corner of the doorway. Peter noticed.

'Em . . .' John mumbled. 'I'm actually on my way out. Give it to me later, yeah?'

'But I always give you your pocket money on a Thursday evening,' Peter reminded him. 'And don't you have homework to do?'

John moved as if he hadn't heard his father, down the stairs, across the hall and out the front door. All the while his right index finger making little rings around his pocket, circling his guilt.

Peter walked back into his bedroom and slumped on the bed. Machiavelli had always been his favourite writer. Peter thought him a misunderstood and demonised author. But until this moment he had not fully understood the meaning of Machiavelli's phrase 'since love and fear cannot coexist, it is safer to be feared than loved'. Peter had always loved his son but, like many men of his generation, he had never shown it.

And what was the result? His son had stolen from him.

The night air grew heavy as Peter stood at the window, thinking about his wife and how everything might have been different if she hadn't left when John was a child. Outside, the last rays of sunlight faded into darkness and along the road streetlights flickered on. All but one.

ANALYSE

This short story works well as a Leaving Certificate composition as it effectively displays awareness of **narrative** shape and remains relevant to the central theme of the title: power and authority in the household. Remember, in the Leaving Certificate examination your short story will be penalised if it deviates from the composition assignment you have chosen.

In the **exposition**, setting is created with detail and **sensory imagery**. A character, Peter, is introduced. He is shown to the reader through action, gesture, body language and **interior monologue**.

The plot begins to unfold, and a second character, John, is introduced. He, too, is shown to the reader. The conflict between Peter and John progresses the plot and **dialogue** is used successfully to show their deteriorating relationship.

In the resolution of the story, **pathetic fallacy** is used to illustrate the emotions of the central character, Peter, and also to encapsulate the atmosphere of the story as a whole.

Narrative WRITING

MAKE

Write **a short story** about a reunion using the following structure as a helping hand.

Opening (1 paragraph): begin your story with a detailed evocation of setting.

Development (3–7 paragraphs): introduce your central character and secondary character; describe and show both of them. The plot of your story is a reunion between these two characters. Include **dialogue** in the interaction between them. Remember that the central focus of your story is a moment of change, or **epiphany**, in your central character.

Conclusion (1 paragraph): use **pathetic fallacy** to illustrate the emotions of the central character and to encapsulate the atmosphere of the story as a whole.

Over to you: Make

Write a short story on any of the following:

1 '. . . I went down the stairs and got my train . . .' ('Reunion')

   Write a short story in which travel plays a significant role in the plot.

2 '. . . he saw two pensive buzzards . . .' ('One of These Days')

   Write a short story set in an unsettling location.

3 'Nearly twenty-five years had passed since then.' ('Household')

   Write a short story in which an experience from the past has a significant impact on the central character.

4 'I followed my father . . .' ('Reunion')

   Write a short story about loyalty.

5 'Monday dawned warm and rainless.' ('One of These Days')

   Write a short story in which the central character is faced with a difficult choice in his or her life.

Remember

Leaving Certificate compositions should be between 750 and 1,000 words. You have ten minutes to plan your composition and one hour to write it. The most important criteria for achieving a good grade are that you write consistently on the title you have chosen and that you use a **register** that suits the **genre** of the title. After that, marks are awarded for good structure and paragraphing, clear and fluent expression, and correct grammar and spelling.

Narrative WRITING

This section offers a useful guide to vocabulary and grammar.

Literary terms and <u>more challenging words</u> have been colour coded throughout this book so that you can use the lists below to quickly and easily find the meaning of any vocabulary you do not understand.

Grammar is considered here under three headings – Agreement, Accuracy and Aptness – and common errors are addressed.

Glossary of literary terms

adjective: a part of speech that typically modifies a **noun** and denotes a quality: a *rousing* speech, a *beautiful* description, a *reflective* essay

adverb: a part of speech that typically modifies a **verb** and adds information about the manner of the action: she spoke *passionately*, they argued *bitterly*; the time of the action: he left *yesterday*; or the location of the action: she walked *ahead*

allegory: from the Greek *allegoria*, which means 'speaking otherwise', this is the term for writing that has a double meaning and that operates on both literal and **symbolic** levels; for example, some critics saw layers of allegory in the film *Avatar*, remarking that the movie's Pandora Woods was a lot like the real Amazon rainforest

alliteration: the repetition of similar sounds in neighbouring words to create a variety of effects; for example, the Prologue of Shakespeare's *Romeo and Juliet* uses alliteration for emphasis and introduction of themes: '*From forth the fatal loins of these two foes / A pair of star-crossed lovers take their life*'

allusion: the use of references to history, mythology, scripture, literature, or popular or contemporary culture to make a point or enhance a description; for example, the phrase 'catch-22' has entered the language to describe a no-win situation, but it is actually an allusion to Joseph Heller's 1961 novel *Catch-22*

analogy: a comparison used to suggest similarity or difference; for example, the film director Baz Luhrman used a comic analogy when he remarked that 'worrying is as effective as trying to solve an algebra equation by chewing bubble-gum'

anecdote: a short, interesting account of an incident or a person, told to introduce or illustrate a point, reveal a truth or capture a character; for example, an amusing literary anecdote tells how the novelist Samuel Butler asked his mother on (what he thought was) her deathbed to promise that she wouldn't let him know if she somehow survived into an after-life, and he suffered dreadfully afterwards, though not from a bad conscience, but merely because his mother recovered; **anecdotal** is the **adjective** used to describe a style or technique that uses anecdotes

auditory: relating to hearing, one of the five senses, and used in criticism to identify the use or evocation of sounds for a variety of effects; for example, in Robert Frost's poem 'Out, Out –' the drama of a fatal accident is created largely through auditory **imagery**: 'The buzz saw snarled and rattled in the yard'

autobiography: an account of a life written by the subject himself or herself; probably the most well-known autobiography is *Diary of a Young Girl* by Anne Frank

biography: an account of a life written by someone other than the subject; two best-selling biographies in recent years have been *Unmasked: The Final Years of Michael Jackson* by Ian Halperin and *Diana: Her True Story* by Andrew Morton

blog: a website on which an individual or a group records opinions and information; some blogs are very influential, for example the Huffington Post

body: in the context of this book, the term refers to the main or central section of a text following the introduction; see **hook**

by-line: line stating the name and often the role of the writer, such as foreign affairs correspondent or chief sports writer

characterisation: the art of creating characters for a **narrative**; when the *Independent* (UK) asked writers in 2005 to list their favourite fictional characters, popular choices included: Tintin, Sherlock Holmes, Gandalf, James Bond, Molly Bloom and Josef K

circular structure: the technique of linking the ending of a text to its beginning, perhaps by returning to complete an **anecdote** or by repeating a quotation. Two novels frequently on the list of prescribed texts for Comparative Study, *Of Mice and Men* by John Steinbeck and *How Many Miles to Babylon?* by Jennifer Johnston, employ a circular structure, beginning and ending in the same place

cliché: an overused word or phrase that has lost all its freshness and most of its meaning; for example, at the end of the day, I hear what you're saying about language, going forward, and the bottom line is, it's not rocket science; see **stereotype**

climax: in a **narrative**, the moment when the crisis reaches its highest point and is afterwards resolved; otherwise, the moment of greatest intensity in a **speech**, in the expression of an emotion, in a description and so on; the punch line in a joke is probably the most common type of narrative climax

colloquial: informal everyday speech, and an essential style for relaxed circumstances such as a talk to classmates and **dialogue** in fiction; for example, 'When I was a kid, my mother had to tie pork chops to my ears so the dog would play with me'

compound word: a word constructed by combining two or more existing words; examples range from the hardly noticeable, such as 'schoolboy', to the more recent, such as 'upscale'

concrete illustration: a specific example, usually given to support a point; for example, 'Terrorism has always been a force in politics; as early as the 1st century, the Sicarii, or "dagger men", assassinated fellow Jewish collaborators with Roman rule by stabbing them in public'

contrast: showing or emphasising difference, usually by **juxtaposition**; for example, 'My mistress' eyes are nothing like the sun; / Coral is far more red, than her lips' red' (Shakespeare's Sonnet 130)

copy: in literary terms, the text in books, magazines and newspapers

debate: a discussion in which opposing arguments are put forward

dialogue: spoken exchanges in a literary work between two or more characters; among the best writers of dialogue are the crime novelist Elmore Leonard, the fantasist Douglas Adams, writer for young adults Judy Blume and the innovative David Foster Wallace

diary: an informal record of a person's life, feelings and reflections; among the most famous diarists are Samuel Pepys (who lived in London during the late seventeenth century and recorded eyewitness accounts of the Great Fire and Great Plague of London), the incomparable Franz Kafka, the founder of analytical psychology Carl Jung and, of course, Anne Frank

didactic: instructive, designed to impart advice, doctrine, lessons or information; under this broad definition, most literature is didactic, but texts that are *specifically* so range from *Works and Days* by Hesiod, c. 700 BCE, to *Sophie's World* by Jostein Gaarder (1991)

ellipsis: the punctuation mark, usually consisting of three periods (. . .), to indicate that words have been omitted, or the deliberate omission of a portion of a story, in both instances with the intention of allowing the reader or viewer to fill in the gaps; it is an essential device in films, where actions such as going from one location to another are rarely shown

emotive: arousing or expressing intense feeling; an effective rhetorical technique used powerfully in Martin Luther King's 'I have a dream' **speech**

epiphany: in literary terms, the moment of insight or revelation that alters a character's world-view

epistolary: taking the form of a letter or letters, including emails and texts; contemporary epistolary novels include *Where Rainbows End* (2006) by the Irish writer Cecelia Ahern, and *Texts from Bennett* (2013) by Mac Lethal, based on the popular Tumblr **blog**

exhortation: urging someone to do, feel or believe something; half-time team **talks** in sporting contests, particularly to the losing side, provide the most common examples of exhortation in today's world

exposition: the opening section of a story, introducing setting, situation and main characters

flashback: an interruption of a **narrative** to return to past events; an unusual use of this popular device occurs in the *Harry Potter* series in the form of a *pensieve*, a stone basin used to store and retrieve memories, in which characters can re-live, not just examine, them

forward moving: advancing or progressing, usually at a brisk pace to generate momentum in an account or a story

frame: any borders that enclose material; in photography, within the image itself (everything else not visible being referred to as being 'outside the frame'); all the events in Emily Brontë's novel *Wuthering Heights* are framed by Mr Lockwood's arrival at and departure from Thrushcross Grange

genre: the French term for a type or category, it is used to describe a group of texts that share certain features; for example, providers of on-demand Internet movies organise films into sub-genres such as western, thriller or comedy

gustatory: relating to taste, one of the five senses, and used in criticism to identify the use or evocation of tastes for a variety of effects; for example, William Carlos Williams's poem 'This Is Just To Say' evokes the taste of plums from the icebox as 'delicious / so sweet / and so cold'

hook: in the context of this book, the term refers to a lively, arresting opening that gets the reader's attention early in a piece of writing such as an article or a short story; see **body**

hyperbole: exaggeration for effect, which, according to the Roman Stoic philosopher Seneca, 'asserts the incredible in order to arrive at the credible'; for example, Gabriel García Márquez, whose story 'One of These Days' is a part of this book, wrote in one of his novels, 'At that time Bogota was a remote, lugubrious city where an insomniac rain had been falling since the beginning of the sixteenth century'; contrast **understatement**

imagery: a general, and rather vague, term for the use of language to evoke sense impressions, best used to describe recurring patterns of **metaphor**; for example, in the Shakespearean plays set for Leaving Certificate, *Macbeth* is dominated by the imagery of blood and darkness, *Othello* by the imagery of magic and illusion, *Hamlet* by the imagery of poison and *King Lear* by the imagery of calculation and suffering; see **metaphor**, **simile**, **symbol**

interior monologue: the representation of a character's inner thoughts, feelings and memories in the sequence in which they occur; for example, in James Joyce's *Ulysses*, which uses the technique extensively, while Leopold Bloom watches a local journalist at a funeral, we are provided with Bloom's interior responses, not the journalist's exterior movements: 'Hynes jotting down something in his notebook. Ah, the names. But he knows them all. No: coming to me.'

irony: according to the Latin author Cicero, this is 'saying one thing and meaning another', and it is generally used to describe an effect where the surface meaning and the deeper meaning are at odds with each other; the most common form of irony is sarcasm in conversation, as when a stupid act is mockingly praised as 'a really bright thing to do'; the adjective is **ironic**

juxtaposition: the arrangement of two or more aspects side by side for the purposes of comparison or **contrast**; in the Japanese verse form the haiku, juxtaposition is the essential skill: 'In the twilight rain / these brilliant-hued hibiscus / A lovely sunset'

memoir: an account of a life written by the subject himself or herself and, according to Gore Vidal, 'how one remembers one's own life', rather than a factual **autobiography**

metaphor: a figurative comparison between things that cannot be literally true, it nonetheless imaginatively implies certain similarities; it is probably the most common of all language skills, since we routinely use metaphor every moment of every day, such as when we employ animal imagery to suggest that a person possesses the good or bad qualities of a rat, a snake, an owl, a lion and so on; see **imagery**, **simile**, **symbol**

modernism: a general, and rather vague, term used to describe an almost universal tendency in the arts in the early twentieth century to move away from the traditional forms and perceptions, such as omniscient **narrative**, into the experimental, such as **interior monologue**

monologue: a speech uttered by one speaker; just as in the **interior monologue**, thoughts, feelings and memories may be included, but the difference here is that the content is delivered aloud

motif: a recurring element in literary works, whether over periods of time (such as the motif of the abandoned child in myth and fairy tale) or woven through an individual work as part of the thematic fabric (such as the motif of insanity in Shakespeare's *King Lear*)

narrative: an account of a sequence of events, told from the beginning (*ab ovo*) or starting from some other point further on (*in media res*)

noun: a part of speech denoting a person, place, thing, creature or idea

objective: an approach that attempts to exclude personal prejudice and bias, resulting in a search for fact supported by evidence that can be independently verified; contrast **subjective**

olfactory: relating to smell, one of the five senses, and used in criticism to identify the use or evocation of odours and aromas for a variety of effects; for example, John Cheever's 'Reunion' brilliantly captures something unsettling about a father whose smell, at noon, was 'a rich compound of whiskey, after-shave lotion, shoe polish, woollens, and the rankness of a mature male'

onomatopoeia: the use of words to imitate the sounds they refer to; comics and graphic novels routinely use this device – POW! SPLLAATT! SWISHHH! – usually with the addition of powerful visual effects; the adjective is **onomatopoeic**

parody: an imitation of another work, in terms of content or style, for the purposes of mocking it. The British comedy group Monty Python created two of the best-known parodies in film with *Monty Python and the Holy Grail* and *Life of Brian*

pathetic fallacy: the error (or fallacy) of attributing human emotions to natural phenomena that have no feelings, usually with the intention of heightening the emotional intensity of a text; the Greek word *pathos* meant 'suffering' and now denotes a feeling of sympathy, and though to call someone 'pathetic' these days would be to insult them, a hundred years ago it complimented a person's sensitivity, the meaning that still survives in 'sympathy', 'empathy' (to enter into another's feelings) and 'apathy' (the absence of strong feelings)

personification: a form of **pathetic fallacy** that attributes human qualities to natural phenomena; for example, Samuel Taylor Coleridge's poem *Christabel* has a leaf as a lone survivor immersed in a death dance: 'The one red leaf, the last of its clan / That dances as often as dance it can'

point of view: who tells the story and from what perspective, and with what motives they do so; the fact that a story changes its reality according to who is telling it was used by the Japanese director Akira Kurosawa in *Rashomon*, a film in which various characters offer conflicting versions of the same incident

prolepsis: foreseeing and forestalling objections to an argument; from the Greek for 'anticipation'

pronoun: a word that substitutes for a **noun** or noun phrase, such as 'I', 'you', 'it', 'they'

HELP IS AT HAND

protagonist: the chief character in a play or story

pun: a play on two words that are similar in sound but have different meanings, intended for humorous effect; some puns are excruciating ('I got a job in a bakery because I kneaded dough'), while others are witty ('John Donne, Anne Donne, Undone' was the poet John Donne's judgement on his elopement with and secret marriage to the love of his life when she was seventeen); many of the greatest writers, including Shakespeare and Dickens, have been addicted to puns

realism: writing that gives the impression of reflecting the realities of life and that strikes the reader as credible and accurate

register: this term is used in the context of the Leaving Certificate examination to describe the use of language appropriate to a particular situation or subject matter; one of the key factors in deciding on a register is the intended audience, since one pitches content, style, tone and vocabulary to suit the audience (it follows from this that the appropriate register includes appropriate content, style, tone and vocabulary)

reportage: the reporting of news or other events, usually in an **objective** manner

reviews: in the context of this book, the term refers to critical assessments of books, films, plays, concerts and so on

rhetorical question: a question asked for persuasive effect rather than to prompt an answer, and often because there is no answer available; for example, Bob Dylan's song 'Blowin' in the Wind' asks a series of rhetorical questions about peace, war and freedom, including 'How many roads must a man walk down?', and although he insisted that the answer was 'blowin' in the wind', the mice in Douglas Adams's comic series *The Hitchhiker's Guide to the Galaxy* maintain that it is '42'

satire: the use of humour, irony, ridicule or exaggeration to expose or criticise the vices, errors and stupidity of humanity; the American writer Ambrose Bierce wrote his satire as a dictionary, *The Devil's Dictionary*, in which he described grammar as 'a system of pitfalls thoughtfully prepared for the feet of the self-made man'; the adjective is **satirical**

sensory: relating to the five senses: hearing, taste, smell, touch, sight; see **auditory**, **gustatory**, **olfactory**, **tactile**, **visual**

sibilance: the recurrence of the hissing sound created by 's', 'sh' and 'z' in a text. One of the best examples is from Edgar Allen Poe's poem 'The Raven': 'And the *s*ilken *s*ad uncertain rustling of each purple curtain'

simile: a phrase that employs 'like' or 'as' to suggest a figurative comparison between things; for example, John Donne's poem 'A Valediction, forbidding mourning' opens in the middle of a simile, 'As virtuous man pass mildly away . . .'; see **imagery**, **metaphor**, **symbol**

speeches: formal addresses delivered to an audience; see **talks**

stereotype: an overused idea or look that has lost its freshness and most of its meaning; see **cliché**

stream of consciousness: the literary method of representing the continuous flow of thoughts, feelings, memories and so on in the mind of a character; see **interior monologue**

subjective: an approach that attempts to include personal perspective and bias, resulting in a view of reality as experienced by the thinking subject and not as an independent thing in itself; contrast **objective**

symbol: anything that is used to represent something beyond itself; for example, = in mathematics and + in road signs; usually the symbol has an unchanging significance, such as the Red Cross and the Red Crescent, whereas the meaning of a **metaphor** changes from context to context; the adjective is **symbolic**

syntax: simply, the arrangement of words in a sentence and the rules that govern these arrangements

tactile: relating to touch, one of the five senses, and used in criticism to identify the use or evocation of physical sensations for a variety of effects; for example, Robert Frost's poem 'The Witch of Coös' contains a vivid description of lying in a cold bed: 'I went to sleep before I went to bed, / Especially in winter when the bed / Might just as well be ice and the clothes snow'

talks: informal addresses delivered to an audience; see **speeches**

triadic structure: any grouping of three ideas, images, names and so on; designed to reinforce a point through repetition with variation

understatement: to make a point in very restrained terms, usually for the sake of **irony** or other impact on the reader; for example, 'This structure has novel features which are of considerable biological interest,' said James Watson and Francis Crick of their discovery of DNA; contrast **hyperbole**

verb: the part of speech used to indicate action, occurrence, the existence of a state and so on; verbs are particularly important in fast-paced **narratives**, as you can see from the following extract from Robert Louis Stevenson's *Kidnapped*: 'Alan, *leaping* back to get his distance, *ran* upon the others like a bull, *roaring* as he went. They *broke* before him like water, *turning*, and *running*, and *falling* one against another in their haste' – the last clause contains an example of **triadic structure**, by the way

visual: relating to sight, one of the five senses, and used in criticism to identify the use or evocation of appearance for a variety of effects; for example, in *Macbeth*, Shakespeare captures how inappropriate the rank of leader looks on a murderous tyrant with a wonderful visual image involving clothes: 'Now does he feel his title / Hang loose about him, like a giant's robe / Upon a dwarfish thief'

Vocabulary

acme: the point of greatest achievement, the peak

aesthetic: concerned with beauty, artistic

affluence: wealth, having a great deal of money

ambiguous: open to more than one meaning or interpretation; the **noun** is **ambiguity**, with plural **ambiguities**

HELP IS AT HAND

androgynous: both male and female in appearance

appraise: assess, evaluate, judge, rate

apt: suitable, fitting, relevant, to the purpose

austerity: severity in financial matters; sternness in personality; but plainness, simplicity and restraint in art

avuncular: literally, resembling an uncle; figuratively, friendly, helpful

blurring: making unclear or indistinct

burlesque: a **parody**; an absurd, comic imitation of something

buzzwords: words that have become trendy or popular with a certain group

camera angle: the location at which a camera is placed to take a shot, for instance high-angle, low-angle, close-up, medium, long and so on – each angle will have a different effect on the viewer

cartography: the science or practice of drawing maps

chiaroscuro: the art of using strong **contrast** between dark and light

chintz: printed cotton fabric with a glazed finish

chronological: in the order of occurrence, calculated in relation to the passage of time

close-up: a camera shot in which the subject is larger than the **frame**, showing much detail; for example, a shot in which only the face of a human being is seen

coda: the conclusion or summary of a literary work

compare: set side by side, juxtapose, liken

composite: combined, blended, mixed

concise: brief, to the point, pithy

confessional: a style of writing that is 'of the personal', the content being **autobiographical** and often exploring subjects considered taboo

connotations: associations, echoes, suggestions

contentious: disputable, debateable (for a point); heated (for a **debate**); quarrelsome (for a person)

contrast: show the difference, dissimilarity

cosmopolitan: international, multiracial (for a place); cultivated or broad-minded (for an outlook)

countenance: face, features (for physical appearance); tolerate, permit (for an action)

criticise: in literary terms, to evaluate and appraise

define: give the meaning of

desolate: barren, deserted, wild (for a place); miserable, anguished (for a person)

diaspora: a dispersion or spreading of people originally belonging to one place or culture

differentiate: to draw a distinction or tell the difference

diminutive: small in stature; a shortened form of a word (for language use)

discourse: discussion, conversation, talk

distinguish: differentiate, tell apart, describe the difference between

dramatise: literally, turn into a play or film; figuratively, make an incident striking or exciting

eclectic: wide ranging, many sided, broad

elicit: bring out, extract

eloquent: having a command of language, fluency, oratory, rhetoric; vividly expressive of an emotion

emphatic: forceful, assertive, unqualified

epigram: proverb, saying, neat turn of phrase, witticism

episodic: intermittent, irregular, sporadic (for general events); in episodes or instalments (for a work of art)

epitome: model, acme, exemplar, essence

erratic: unpredictable, inconsistent, irregular, unstable

evaluate: assess, appraise, put a value on, estimate the worth of

evocative: suggestive, expressive, moving, poignant

evoke: bring to mind, conjure up; the **noun** is **evocation**

fey: giving the impression of vague mystery

formative: impressionable (for the age of a person); determining (for an influence)

formulate: draw up, work out (a plan), prepare

framing: any technique used to contain and focus on a subject

gilded: literally, covered with gold; figuratively, splendid, embellished

guise: external appearance, persona

hankering: longing, yearning

homage: tribute, respect; to honour or pay tribute to

iconic: achieving the status of an icon, an idol, a model

illustrious: distinguished, renowned, celebrated, brilliant

impact: in literary terms, the impression a work makes or the influence it has

incongruous: out of place, unsuitable, incompatible

indolent: idle, languid, lazy, listless

inscrutable: mysterious, enigmatic, impossible to interpret

interpret: explain, elucidate, make clear the meaning or effect of

intertextuality: the relationships between separate literary texts

intuitive: instinctive, non-rational understanding

linguistic: language-producing, verbal

listlessness: lethargy, languor, idleness, indolence

long shot: a camera shot in which an entire figure is shown in relation to its surroundings; commonly referred to as a 'wide shot' these days

lucidity: clarity, sharpness, brightness

ludicrous: ridiculous, laughable, foolish

maelstrom: turmoil, confusion, whirl

malingering: slacking, pretending to be ill, shamming

melancholic: sad, sorrowful, disconsolate, glum

melancholy: sadness, glumness, low spirits

meticulous: thorough, painstaking, precise

mid-shot: a camera shot in which the subject is seen from a medium distance; also called a 'medium shot'

minutiae: details, finer points, trifles

montage: a technique in film-making in which a series of short shots are edited into a sequence, either to indicate the passage of time, or (in Soviet cinema) to create **symbolic** meaning

narcissistic: adoring, admiring, being in love with, or being obsessed with, oneself

neologism: new word, newly coined term or phrase, invented expression

nostalgia: longing for the past, wistful remembrance of the past; the adjective is **nostalgic**

obsequiousness: being fawning, grovelling or submissive

oligarchic: relating to an oligarchy, which is government or control by a small group of people

omniscient: knowing everything

opulent: luxurious, rich, splendid, abundant

paraphrase: express in one's own words, rephrase

pensive: thoughtful, reflective, introspective

persona: image, character, personality, mask, <u>guise</u>, external appearance

pinioned: held down, restrained

pithy: <u>concise</u>, compact, short and sweet, to the point

plagiarism: copying, infringement of copyright, theft

posturing: posing, striking an attitude

probity: integrity, honesty, truthfulness

props: the shortened form of 'stage properties', generally anything distinct from the humans and the setting in a photograph, film shot or stage scene

rancour: bitterness, spite, hate, malice

rapport: affinity, bond, harmony, sympathy

resonate: strike a chord, echo, <u>evoke</u>

Riemann's zeta function: complex function in analytic number theory with applications in physics, probability and statistics

ruckus: ruction, disturbance

ruefully: regretfully, sorrowfully

self-deprecating: not over-valuing oneself, used in humour and other forms of communication to aid audience identification

solicitation: demands, requests

solitude: isolation, seclusion

spectre: ghost, spirit, shadow

subterranean: below the surface of the earth

superlative: expression insisting that something excels all others and is of the highest possible quality

syllable: a single vowel sound, there being two in *vowel* and three in *syllable*

taboo: forbidden, illegal, unacceptable, not spoken about

totalitarian: authoritarian, tyrannical, repressive

transience: impermanence, briefness, temporariness

transitory: temporary, impermanent, brief

trepidation: fear, apprehension, dread, uneasiness

truism: maxim, cliché, stock phrase

ubiquitous: being everywhere at once

unequivocal: clear cut, unqualified, positive, unmistakeable, un<u>ambiguous</u>

urbane: sophisticated, cultivated, polished

vitiate: make faulty, pervert, corrupt

whimsical: playful, mischievous

wry: *ironic*, **satirical**, witty, humorous

Grammar

> This syllabus aims at initiating students into enriching experiences with language so that they become more adept and thoughtful users of it and more critically aware of its power and significance in their lives.
>
> Leaving Certificate HL English Syllabus

In line with the syllabus, this book seeks to help you become more adept in using language for the purposes of self-expression and communication. Grammar is an aid to self-expression and communication, not a set of stand-alone rules. In exploring grammar, therefore, the objective is not to learn a set of regulations that, somehow or other, you will remember to stick to while talking or writing; the objective is to make yourself familiar with usage that improves self-expression and communication and with usage that hinders self-expression and communication.

Grammar is considered here under three headings – Agreement, Accuracy and Aptness – and the most common errors made by students are addressed.

Agreement

Can you identify the error(s) in each of the following sentences?

1. It's funny how we start off in life as a carefree child.
2. The excitement and anticipation was pumping in my veins.
3. It sits in the back of our minds waiting for the person that pushes you over the edge.
4. As a youth both my sister and I would visit my grandmother after school.
5. I was standing in the dark when all of a sudden the crowd begins to roar.
6. The wind was whipping the rain against your face, but as I got closer I could hear thousands of people.
7. Everybody's craniums are impressive.
8. He walks into the classroom, sits down, took out a can of deodorant, sprayed the back of the guy in front of him, and walks out again.
9. Yesterday, after I picked up the car the day before, I drove it to the garage, I took it out again.
10. I felt cheated, and you are angry at that, it's the sort of thing one hates.

If one part of a sentence disagrees with another part, the resulting argument gets ugly. Each of the above sentences is ugly. Example 1 claims that we is a carefree child, 4 that a brother and sister are one person, 8 that human beings can simultaneously act in the present and in the past, and so on. Possibly the most confusing is sentence 7, which seems to suggest that each human being has more than one brain and also that there are a few communal brains that somehow belong to us all. These claims are absurd, as well as ungainly.

The recurring problem is inconsistency. Let's look at each in turn:

1 The **pronoun** 'we' is plural, but the **noun** 'child' is singular. *We start off as a child?* No. *We start off as children.*

2 The combination of the nouns 'excitement' and 'anticipation' is plural (two things), but the **verb** 'was' is singular. *Two people was absent?* No. *Two people were absent.*

3 The first pronoun 'our' is first person plural, but the second pronoun 'you' is second person singular. *Our minds is your mind?* No. *Our minds are ours.*

4 The indefinite article and noun 'a youth' is singular, but the combination of noun and pronoun 'my sister and I' is plural. *My sister and I were a youth?* No. *My sister and I were youths.*

5 The first verb 'was standing' is in the past tense, but the second verb 'begins' is in the present tense. *I stood and begins to talk?* No. *I stood and began to talk.*

6 The first pronoun 'your' is second person singular, but the second pronoun 'I' is first person singular. *I smile with your lips?* No. *I smile with my lips.*

7 The indefinite pronoun 'everybody' is singular, but the verb 'are' and noun 'craniums' are plural. *Everybody were impressive?* No. *Everybody was impressive.*

8 The first and second verbs ('walks' and 'sits') are present tense, the third and fourth verbs ('took' and 'sprayed') are past tense and the final verb ('walks') is present tense again. *He walks and sprayed?* No. *He walks and sprays.* Or: *He walked and sprayed.*

9 All three verbs ('picked', 'drove' and 'took') are past tense, giving the impression that everything happened on the same day, even though the adverbs 'yesterday' and 'the day before' indicate that two consecutive days were involved. The result is confusing. *After I gone I returned?* No. *After I had gone, I returned. Yesterday, after I had picked up the car the day before and driven it to the garage, I took it out again.*

10 The first pronoun 'I' is first person, the second pronoun 'you' is second person and the third pronoun 'one' is indefinite. *I lifted the cup with your hands?* No. *I lifted the cup with one's hands?* No. *I lifted the cup with my hands.*

As you can see, if the sentences are simplified, the errors become obvious. Learn from this exercise. If you are having problems with grammar, simplify your style, keep your sentences short and express yourself directly.

Another reason for poor grammar is lack of planning. Good writers map a sentence in the mind before physically beginning it. Error-prone writers start sentences without knowing how to end them. In many of the above examples, you can see where the writer lost control of the sentence. *The wind was whipping the rain against your face* (pause, wonder what to write next, decide it's about getting to the gig, which you can hear before you reach it, so put down) *but as I got closer I could hear thousands of people.* By the time the writer begins the second half of the sentence, he or she has forgotten what is in the first half.

Accuracy

If you misplace punctuation marks, you change or obscure the meaning of an expression. You may even express the opposite of what you intend. Can you identify the error(s) in each of the following sentences and signs?

1 Let's eat children!
2 Its difficult for a lioness to abandon it's cub.
3 My only sisters' friend wrote his three sister's names.
4 'I think it's the best thing to do. He said.
5 Woman without her man is nothing.
6 Children drive slowly.
7 The defendant said his barrister has a history of drug abuse.
8 Frozen Margarita's Draft Beer
9 Black-cab drivers come under attack.
10 Fresh pea's, new seasons carrots and grilled aubergine's.

Each of the above expressions either obscures or distorts the intended meaning. Example 1 exhorts us to become cannibals, and although Jonathan Swift's great satire *A Modest Proposal* suggests with savage irony that this is what society does to the children of the poor, neither **satire** nor **irony** is intended here; 7 claims that the defendant represents the barrister in court and that the barrister is the criminal; 9 maintains that only the drivers of black cabs are vulnerable; and so on. These claims are absurd, and for the most part laughable.

The recurring problem is incorrect punctuation. Let's look at each in turn:

1 Unless you put a comma (,) after 'eat', indicating that you are addressing the children, the noun 'children' becomes the object of the verb 'eat', as 'stones' becomes the object of the verb 'break' in 'Let's break stones!' *Let's eat children!* Surely not. *Let's eat, children!*
2 The apostrophe (') is misused twice, making it more difficult at first reading to understand the sense. The first 'Its' is a contraction of the verb form 'It is' and because one letter has been removed and the remaining letters have been squeezed together, these changes must be marked with an apostrophe: *It's*. The second 'its' is not a verb and not a contraction, but a possessive pronoun, and so does not require an apostrophe: *its*.
3 Again, the apostrophe (') is misused twice, making it more difficult at first reading to understand the sense. The first 'sister' is singular, since there's only one – so, *sister's* – whereas the second 'sister' is plural because there are three of them: *sisters'*.
4 **Dialogue** is wrongly presented; it should be *'I think it's the best thing to do,' he said.*
5 This is a popular and entertaining demonstration of how punctuation can change meaning because *Woman: without her, man is nothing* claims that men are dependent on women, whereas *Woman, without her man, is nothing* claims that women are dependent on men.
6 It might, or might not, come as a relief to worried parents to learn that children drive more carefully than adults, but the message here should be a caution to adult drivers: *Children! Drive slowly!*

7 As written, the sentence claims that, according to the defendant, the barrister had a history of drug abuse. Look again at 4 above, and particularly at the placement of the comma in reporting speech. *The defendant, said his barrister, has a history of drug abuse.* Or even more clearly, *'The defendant,' said his barrister, 'has a history of drug abuse.'*

8 As written, the sign seems to suggest that there's a brewer called Margarita, who is frozen, but still produces draft beer. Business signs are particularly prone to the misused apostrophe, so much so that the error has become known as grocer's apostrophe. This one should read *Frozen Margaritas,* (one type of drink available) *Draft Beer* (another type of drink available). See 10 also.

9 The hyphen (-) is misused. It may well be that drivers of black cabs are more vulnerable than the drivers of all other cabs, but that is not the intended meaning here. The intention is to highlight incidents of racism: *Black cab-drivers come under attack*.

10 Multiple examples of grocer's apostrophe; it should be: *Fresh peas, new season's carrots and grilled aubergines*. The plural of a noun (peas, aubergines) never needs an apostrophe.

Aptness

Slackness in expression draws attention to itself. It may not change the intended meaning, but it will distract focus from it. Can you identify the error(s) in each of the following sentences?

1 She stroked her hair, removing the damp moisture.

2 I cringed inwardly to myself.

3 The most scariest thing in the world is a spider.

4 Myself and my older brother started jumping.

5 Me, being small, was picked on.

6 My experience with money would tend to be good.

7 I would listen to their album over and over until my ears would bleed.

8 At the young age of four my mother sent me to piano lessons.

9 The stroll to school seemed ten times longer than the walk home.

10 After what seemed like an eternity in a taxi with an extremely patriotic Roman driver who couldn't contain his excitement for 'beautiful Roma' and insisted on explaining every inch of ground we covered to which I replied with a half smile to match my half-closed eyes.

Good writing directs the reader by means of carefully chosen language and **syntax**, which is the arrangement of words and phrases to create well-formed sentences. Each of the above examples fails to do this and instead encourages the reader to wander off into irrelevancies. Example 1 invites the reader to pause and wonder if he or she has ever encountered *dry* moisture; 9 gives the wrong impression *twice*; and 10 traps the reader in a bewildering labyrinth.

The recurring problem is inapt, or inappropriate, expression. The first three suffer from overwriting, that is, the use of redundant, unnecessary words:

1   Since moisture is, by definition, damp, the first sentence should be much neater and have a cleaner impact: *She stroked her hair, removing the moisture.*

2   Since you cannot cringe outwardly, or perform any inner response outwardly for the benefit of others, the second sentence should be beautifully simple: *I cringed.*

3   Since scariest *is* the most (scary), the third sentence should also be crisper: *The scariest thing in the world is a spider.*

The remarkable ugliness of examples 4 and 5 can be exposed by removing the inessential parts and considering the basic information in each case:

4   *Myself started jumping* – who would write such nonsense? The answer is authors who place extra material between the pronoun and the verb instead of keeping them close together. It should be: *My older brother and I started jumping.*

5   To avoid saying *Me was picked on*, this sentence should be restructured: *Being small, I was picked on.*

Examples 6 and 7 illustrate the very common error of misusing the conditional tense of a verb ('would') instead of the simple present tense ('is') or simple past tense ('was'). The conditional is so called because it always depends on some extra condition: *If I had worked, I would have earned money.* As a general rule, never use 'would' without 'if':

6   This sentence is unwieldy and unpleasant to read. *My experience with money tends to be good* is much more effective because of its accuracy.

7   Similarly, *I listened to their album over and over until my ears bled* is a much better sentence.

8   This example has a wandering phrase, 'at the young age of four'. We might ask if there was ever an *old* age of four, but we have more important concerns. A phrase (that is, a group of words that act as a part of speech but cannot stand alone as a sentence) will always attach itself to the nearest noun, pronoun or verb. In this case, the nearest is 'my mother'. *At the young age of four my mother?* Surely she was older than four when she sent you to piano lessons? Try: *I wasn't much older than four when my mother first sent me to piano lessons.* Or: *At the tender age of four, I was sent to piano lessons by my mother.* As a general rule, ensure that there is nothing between a phrase and what it refers to.

9   This sentence provides an example of selecting the right words, but putting them in the wrong places. Surely a 'walk' is much more demanding than a 'stroll' and feels longer because it is not as enjoyable: *The walk to school seemed ten times longer than the stroll home.*

10 As already mentioned, good writers map a sentence in the mind before physically beginning it. Error-prone writers start sentences without knowing how to end them. Example 10, despite its incredible length, is not a complete sentence. The writer has become lost and is unable to find the way back out. The solution is to write shorter sentences. They're much more effective. *I spent what seemed like an eternity in a taxi. The driver was an extremely patriotic Roman. He couldn't contain his excitement for 'bella Roma'. He insisted on explaining every inch of ground we covered. Most of the time, my eyes were half-closed. Most of the time, I replied with a matching half-smile. When we finally arrived at my destination . . .*